GLYNN CHRISTIAN
TASTES
Royal
THAILAND

WITH PHOTOGRAPHS
BY
JULIET PIDDINGTON

BBC BOOKS

Glynn Christian has been cooking on television since 1980, making over 1000 live appearances in such popular shows as *Pebble Mill at One*, Cilla Black's *Surprise, Surprise* and *Noel Edmonds' Roadshow*. He helped launch the BBC's *Breakfast Time* and has made cookery series on location in New Zealand, California, Sri Lanka and China as well as programmes on microwave cookery and the history of afternoon tea.

Amongst almost 30 books, his best known are *The Delicatessen Food Handbook*, described as 'one of the only 10 books you need', *Edible France*, a guide to what rather than where to eat in France, and *Fragile Paradise*, the only biography of his great great great great grandfather Fletcher Christian, leader of the mutiny on Bounty in 1789.

This book is published to accompany the television series entitled *Glynn Christian Tastes Royal Thailand* which was first broadcast in 1997. The series was produced by Glynn Christian Productions Limited for the BBC.

Published by BBC Books,
an imprint of BBC Worldwide Publishing,
BBC Worldwide Limited, Woodlands,
80 Wood Lane, London W12 0TT

First published 1997
© Glynn Christian 1997

ISBN 0 563 38766 1

Photographs: Juliet Piddington
Home Economist: Sarah Ramsbottom

Printed in Great Britain by Cambus Litho Ltd, East Kilbride
Bound in Great Britain by Hunter & Foulis Ltd, Edinburgh
Colour separations by Radstock Reproductions Ltd, Midsomer Norton
Cover printed by Belmont Press, Northampton

CONTENTS

INTRODUCTION

Oh, what a joy! A classic cuisine without classic recipes. Unlike the cuisines of Europe, Thai cookery has virtually no recipes carved in stone. Here novelty, individuality and experimentation are encouraged and admired, for this is a cuisine meant to titillate and stimulate, to surprise and delight when sultry weather makes appetites and palates jaded and sullen. Thus when you hear someone describe a restaurant as cooking 'authentic' Thai food, they merely mean Thai food that they like. Only Thai ingredients can be authentic: the dishes are not meant to be. Yet underlying such apparent freedom there is, of course, a firm set of rules.

Thais generally eat one main meal at night and spend the rest of the day snacking or enjoying one-dish meals, which are often noodle-based. The classic full Thai meal is centred on rice, as you might expect, and once would also have included a fried and a steamed dish, a curry, a soup, a salad, and a selection of desserts, including fresh fruit. These busier days, it is more likely that the rice will only be accompanied by three or so dishes.

Whatever the number of dishes, they are served pretty much at the same time, with no true distinction between appetizers and main courses. Soups, for instance, are supped throughout a meal – for the sake of contrast as well as keeping up the liquid intake. Thai salads are served neither as appetizers nor as palate cleansers between courses, but are also eaten throughout the meal and, unlike their Western equivalents, they are dressed with sharp and fragrant liquids rather than oils and vinegars.

The object, whether the choice is big or small, is to provide a well-planned and executed balance of sour and sweet, bitter, acid and hot, with plenty of different textures too, many of which are quite foreign to the West's palate. This extraordinary variety is commonly lost on Western diners because they eat Thai food incorrectly, and, equally incorrectly, think it should be fiercely hot.

Traditionally, Thais ate with their fingers and many still do. The polite and proper way to eat was to gather a portion of rice and to add to that a portion of one or another dish, enjoying the combination of rice and other flavours, dish by dish. Thus meat, poultry, fish and vegetables were cut small so that the amount your fingertips could politely contain with rice could be put into your mouth in a seemly manner. You never mixed the dishes, either on your plate or on your palate. Main dishes never were – and never should be – eaten alone but always with rice, mouthful by mouthful. Without rice to balance it, the flavour will be too strong.

Today, spoons and forks have replaced fingertips, but the same rules apply. A spoonful or mouthful should have about equal proportions of rice and an accompanying dish, the rice providing a delicate, bland background and a dilution of the stronger flavours. It is utterly incorrect to eat a mouthful of anything but a soup or dessert without also including the rice. It is worse, incidentally, to eat from your fork – about as bad manners as it would be for us to eat off our knife.

And then there are chillies. Essentially the more chillies you eat, the less effect they have. Food which is hot to you as a visitor in Thailand or at an occasional Thai restaurant will not taste hot to regular local or daily diners. Thai food in general is not scarily hot to Thais, but pleasantly piquant. If you only eat chillies occasionally, an effect of extreme heat in your mouth means you are experiencing an utterly false taste which masks the real reason you should be eating Thai food. It is entirely acceptable to ask for little or no chilli in a Thai restaurant, or to cook modestly with them. This will assure you of a taste closer to what Thais experience. In any case there are plenty of Thais who don't like chilli, so you will not be thought of as a sissy – quite the reverse! People with developed palates will admire you for wanting to taste the full spectrum of ingredients and a good chef will find you doubly worth cooking for.

But if there are no real recipes and Thai food is not necessarily hot, what should it taste like? Think voluptuous fragrances, think elegance, think multiple nuances of flavour that can continue for ages after you swallow. Thai cooks use possibly more ingredients than cooks of any other nationality, particularly raw ingredients, many of which are still gathered from streets, fields, rivers and banks. Yet they are underpinned with a few basic flavours which are unique to Thai cookery.

The most important is a trinity of garlic, black pepper and coriander root – this is the only cuisine which relies so heavily on the root of this, the most widely used herb in the world. Pounded together in this or that proportion, the Thai trinity was probably the original Thai curry base, relying on the flavoursome heat of peppercorns, which they call Thai pepper, for a hot sensation, as did Sri Lankans and many others before the chilli arrived from South America with Portuguese travellers. Three types of basil are used too and in such a combination the citric casts of their essentially aniseed flavours add wonderfully deep flavour perspectives.

Many writers point out that perhaps the burgeoning popularity of Thai food is due to the bright, sharp combination which finalises many dishes: sliced chillies and fresh lime juice. But if these are all you taste, the dish is considered vulgar by those who really know. If you can't taste all the other ingredients you have wasted money and the cook has wasted time.

In the south of Thailand, coconut milk and cream are used extensively and they rather soften the harsher flavour base of the area. They are rarely used in the north, because coconuts are scarcer. Food in the extreme south and the north-east is chilli hot, a geographical divide which can be explained socially and economically. Essentially, chilli is a refuge of the poor, worldwide, used to give mouth sensation (it is a trauma rather than a flavour) and gratification where there is little food, or none of great interest. By burning the palate chilli encourages the brain to release endorphins which give a physical sense of well-being. Of course you use increasingly large amounts, for it gives you the sensations that your food cannot, if you are poor or if your land is not productive.

Make no mistake, chillies can become a true addiction. Their over-use gives an unbalanced appreciation of food and can develop into a self-destructive need for chillies at the expense of everything else on the plate. This can be avoided by proper understanding of their use. In a society where a good variety of good-tasting food can be taken for granted, chillies should be used only as a background, for piquancy and contrast, never as the predominant effect. If that is what you want close this book immediately and then spread chilli sauce onto sliced white bread ...

In the central plains, Bangkok and other bigger centres, life – and palates – are different. Rich alluvial plains not only provide plenty of rice but also grow massive amounts of fresh produce all year round. There is plenty to eat and plenty of variety – pleasure comes without pain. It was here that the court and its associated nobles created a style of food that is even more sophisticated and gentler in flavour, truly more refined. Call it royal, palace or noble food, this elegant tradition in Thai cookery might easily be thought of as an equivalent of the *haute cuisine* of Europe, but they have nothing in common. *Haute cuisine* is as far removed from every-day eating as it is possible to imagine, entirely different dishes cooked only by professionals in professional establishments, usually based on stocks which are monumentally expensive and time-consuming.

Royal Thai food comprises basically the same dishes which are enjoyed by the rest of the country, though they are richer, finer and more decorated. Where a villager might use pork, a palace might use more expensive prawns, and then cook in butter rather than oil. The techniques will be more refined and the presentation may be alarmingly elaborate: a veritable gallery of intricately carved fruit and flowers, arranged flowers, orchards, buds and leaves, different for every dish.

Once only noble and royal households had the time to present food so beautifully, but in the modern world the once precious and hidden secrets have been more widely shared. The food served in most Thai restaurants in most countries of the world is actually a modern amalgam of rural, citified and palace food – peasant food decorated regally. It is none the worse for that, but you should not expect carved fruits and vegetables to accompany food anywhere but in restaurants or in nobler houses. That is to say, you are not failing in your duty if you do not spend hours carving decorations for your dinner: these were originally only done by women of the palace to fill their interminable hours of luxurious imprisonment.

As regards quantities, it would be foolish and unkind of me to tell you anything but the truth. The number of servings given for each recipe in this book varies enormously. If you are serving Western-style meals, course by course and perhaps even without rice, then most recipes will serve 2–4 people as a single course. Perhaps it is simpler to look at the quantity of main ingredients in each recipe: in broad terms, 125–200 g/4–6 oz of meat, poultry or fish is considered an average serving, particularly if you serve extra vegetables. If you are greedier, increase quantities proportionally.

If you are serving in the authentic Thai-style, with equal quantities of rice and other dishes, these dishes will serve 4–6 people. But if you dine more multiculturally, with all the dishes on the table and proportionally less rice than a Thai person might serve, 4 is perhaps nearer the mark. An excellent way to plan is to serve one dish per diner plus one other, plus rice, decreasing the ratio as the numbers increase. Thus dinner for 3 would comprise 4 dishes with rice, while 6 people might need the equivalent of 6 dishes with rice (I say equivalent because you may wish to double up on quantities rather than cooking 6 different dishes).

Of course, you can use these recipes any way you wish. But please remember all these recipes improve by being eaten with rice. If not, reduce the amounts of all flavouring, not just the chilli, to take account of this and then you can really taste the extraordinary flavours of Thailand.

A–Z OF THAI INGREDIENTS

The range of ingredients used in Thailand is gigantic, greater I think even than that of China. But I have tried to use only those which are relatively easily available or for which there are simple substitutes. Thus, the following guide is only to the ingredients found in this book, a starting point for exploration of this most fascinating of cuisines.

Aubergine: From tiny ones shaped like peas to long, thin, purple ones, all the Thai aubergines have the distinct advantage of not needing to be disgorged of bitter juices. Thus, choose whatever kind is available. Tiny cubes of a white-fleshed, purple-streaked aubergine are just as acceptable as pea aubergines.

Bamboo shoots: Use canned ones, but rinse them well. They need no additional cooking.

Banana leaves: The thick-ribbed leaves of the banana plant – actually a herb rather than a tree, as it has no trunk – are extremely useful if you can get them. They make wondrous serving platters or linings for your own plates but must always be lightly oiled for the sake of appearances. Best of all, bannana leaves make wonderful wrappings for food, whether you are steaming, microwaving, grilling or roasting. Oil the leaves first and use them shinier, upper side outside. You may need to fix them with cocktail sticks sometimes.

Bananas: The variety most favoured in Thailand for a wide range of desserts is the *kluay nam wha*. But, as there are thirty or more named varieties for the Thais to chose from, they enjoy the luxury of a choice we do not. We must make do with whatever short, fat variety of banana is available, even the tiny ones known as Lady Fingers, as long as they are ripe and sweet. South American or Caribbean fruit will do, but they must be really ripe, with spotty skins, a luscious smell and a sweetness not marred by even a hint of acidity

Basil: Although three types of basil are used in Thailand, the distinction between them is not so great that recipes will be ruined by substitutions. Sweet basil, *horapha*, is closest to the European variety and is used lavishly. In most cases, you can use the fresh basil you buy without a second thought.

The basil variety called *kaprow* in Thai is often referred to as 'holy basil'; its leaves are thinner and sometimes tinged with red. Holy basil is not used as much as is generally thought, for it must be cooked and only appears with dishes based on meat, poultry or fish. *Manglak* is the variety closest to the bush basil of Italy and can be used lavishly as both an ingredient and a garnish; it has a sharper taste that some think of as lemony, minty or peppery

Celery: In Thai cookery, this means the very highly flavoured stalks of celeriac. Unless you grow your own, finding a celeriac root with some of its green top intact can be difficult but, using celery leaf and the thinnest of the new stalks, you will get very close to the flavour.

Chillies: Firstly, I must emphasise that Thai food does not taste hot to most Thais. When you eat chillies daily, the effect becomes less and less. Thus the reputation of food in Thailand and the reality are quite different. In any case, there are plenty of Thais who do not like chilli at all or who ask for only a small amount. Only one thing is certain: the chilli effect should never get in the way of the other flavours of a dish; if you experience only heat, or more heat than flavour, the dish is unbalanced and thus badly prepared.

For those who eat Thai or other chilli-flavoured food only rarely, the rule must be to use extreme restraint, or to cook without them altogether and to add piquancy by dipping into a chilli sauce or sprinkling with Tabasco sauce.

The general rule about potency is the inverse to expectation. The smaller the chilli, the hotter it is likely to be. Unripe green ones are usually more intense than riper red ones but this is balanced by the precise amount of each which is used. The most explosive of chillies are called *prik khee nu*, which roughly translates as mouse droppings; they are only about 1 cm (½ inch) long. Beyond that, major differences in heat and what flavour there is will often be more imaginary than anything else; feel free to use whatever you can buy.

(OVERLEAF) *Some of the fresh ingredients required for Thai cookery*

9

Coriander

Thai shallots

Kaffir lime
and leaves

Fresh noodles

Galangal

Black peppercorns

Garlic

Basil

Turmeric root

Spring onion

Ginger

Krachai

Thai aubergines

Green peppercorns

Beansprouts

Chillies

Chillies

Thai aubergine

Lemon grass

Taste before you go too far and remember that by removing the seeds and/or inner membranes of chillies you can reduce the effect; you will soon judge what is right for you and your family.

Fresh chillies – whether with or without their fiery seeds and inner membranes, fresh chillies will be less potent if sliced, more potent if pounded or crushed. In general, they are used in one of those ways when cooked in a dish, but sliced lengthways, in what we would call *julienne* strips, to avoid the seeds, when used as a garnish.

Dried chillies – because the dried chillies used in Thailand are fairly big, they are *relatively* less hot than expected, hence the astonishingly large number called for in some recipes. The small dried chillies which come commercially packed in most British stores are hotter; if these are what you must use, fewer would possibly be better in recipes in which chillies are specified by number.

Dried chillies are generally soaked in warm water for 5 minutes before the top is removed and the seeds washed out; sometimes the soaking water is incorporated in the dish and sometimes those of rugged palate will include the seeds too.

Chilli jam – this is easy to make or to purchase and a very useful ingredient to spice up your cookery, Thai or otherwise. It is made by frying together a couple of tablespoons each of sliced garlic and Thai shallots and 6–8 chillies, until they are golden brown. Pound or process these to a paste, with 6 generous tablespoons of dried shrimps, soaked in water; then flavour to taste with a couple of tablespoons of *nam pla* (fish sauce) and up to twice that amount of palm sugar. Fry this into a homogenous and fragrant state in a few tablespoons of oil and then store it in an air-tight bottle or jar.

Coconut milk and cream: Once you had to make these yourself, with freshly grated or desiccated coconut. These days, both are available in most good supermarkets as concentrates, simply reconstituted by adding water. You will also find them canned and, in some speciality shops, in the freezer cabinets; beware of these as they are sometimes already sweetened. You probably know already, but it is worth pointing out that the liquid contained in a coconut is actually coconut water, and virtually useless in the kitchen.

Condiments: When you are dining in company, it is good manners to make food with only a light chilli content but then to offer condiments with which individual preferences can be sustained. At the most basic, serve chillies sliced into vinegar, lime juice or tamarind water; a more complicated version is made by adding garlic, crushed peppercorns, *nam pla* (fish sauce) or palm sugar as well. A variety of pickled vegetables, bowls or bottles of *nam pla* (fish sauce), some salt, soy sauce, sweet chilli sauce and palm sugar might all find their way on to the table, once you know what you or your family and friends like. It's up to you, really!

Coriander: Also called cilantro and Chinese parsley, the unique flavour of coriander leaf makes it the most widely used herb in the world, even though it is said to have precisely the same smell as crushed bed bugs. It's endemic (epidemic if you hate it) to cuisines as different as those of South America and China and can easily be overused as a garnish, boringly making every dish taste the same. Thai cookery makes coriander overkill even more likely, as it efficiently also uses the root of the plant (Thailand is one of the very few countries which does this). The root is combined with black pepper and garlic as the cuisine's single most telling imprint: an essential trinity of the Thai kitchen.

Unfortunately, even though coriander plants are usually sold with their roots intact (the way to differentiate it from flat-leaf parsley) the roots are very small compared to those sold in Thailand. You should use chopped whole plants as a substitute, including the stalks and leaves as well as the root.

Curry pastes: You don't have to make your own, but don't expect commercial pastes to taste the same. If you do have to use them, realize that citric acid or vinegar might have been used as a preservative and that the more expensive and more fragrant ingredients are likely to have been skimped on (with the exception, perhaps, of Charmaine Solomon's range). The trick is to add extra fresh ingredients, if you can.

You can argue forever about the differences between red and green curries, because either one can be hotter than the other, depending on how many chillies you choose to use. But essentially, even though they are based pretty much on the same ingredients, the green one generally uses a greater proportion of coriander, lemon grass, galangal and kaffir lime, the fragrant rather than spicy flavours: I have made it with very little chilli indeed and found it remarkably delicious. You can, if you like, even use exactly the same base and merely change the chilli colour, as I have seen. More than ever, it is entirely up to you.

Pounding in a mortar and pestle does give superior results, as the oils and flavourings really do mingle. If you have to use a food processor, try to give the mixture a pounding afterwards, even if in small amounts at a time; it is also a help to have deep-frozen the lemon grass, lime leaves and galangal, because this breaks them down and makes them easier to process into a paste. The pastes can be stored for a couple of months in the refrigerator or for longer in the freezer, in which case, make pellets of 2 or 3 tablespoons each (the usual recipe quantity) by freezing in an ice-cube tray.

Here are two versions of each, to show the variation and to encourage you to experiment. For other styles of curry pastes , see individual recipes.

GREEN CURRY PASTE 1
Nam Prik Kaung Kheaw Whan

This is from The Oriental Hotel and makes enough for four or more dishes. Because this curry paste is intended to be quite hot, I have suggested that you don't discard the seeds in the chillies. However, this decision depends solely on personal taste, as does the variation, up or down, of the number of chillies used: you might like to begin by using far fewer green chillies.

MAKES ABOUT 12 TABLESPOONS

12 small green chillies, chopped
2 Thai shallots, chopped
4 garlic cloves, chopped
4 cm (1½ inch) piece of fresh
galangal, chopped
1 tablespoon chopped coriander root
or plant
4–6 tablespoons chopped lemon grass
stalks

1 teaspoon chopped kaffir lime zest
10 black peppercorns
½ teaspoon coriander seeds, roasted
and ground
¼ teaspoon cumin seeds, roasted and
ground
2 teaspoons kapi (shrimp paste)
6 tablespoons vegetable oil

Pound or process together the chillies, shallots, garlic, galangal, coriander root and lemon grass. Add the lime zest, peppercorns, coriander and cumin seeds, plus the kapi, and continue until you have a smooth paste. Gradually work in the oil until you have a homogenous paste. Transfer to air-tight storage jars.

This paste can be kept in the refrigerator for a long period, but ensure the lid is well sealed.

GREEN CURRY PASTE 2

The second recipe, from The Thai House, actually uses even more chillies to make only about half the quantity, and uses proportionally less of the fragrant ingredients, too. This will make enough for three or four dishes.

MAKES ABOUT 8 TABLESPOONS

15 hot green chillies
3 tablespoons chopped Thai shallots
1 tablespoon chopped garlic
1 teaspoon chopped fresh galangal
1 tablespoon chopped lemon grass
½ teaspoon chopped kaffir lime zest
1 teaspoon chopped coriander root or plant

5 white peppercorns
1 tablespoon coriander seeds, roasted and ground
1 teaspoon cumin seeds, roasted and ground
1 teaspoon salt
1 teaspoon kapi (shrimp paste)

Pound or process together all the ingredients. Store in a well-sealed jar in the refrigerator. That's it!

RED CURRY PASTE 1
Nam Prik Kaeng Daeng

The first recipe, from The Oriental, not only includes the turmeric of the north but also the cinnamon of southern curries. Either or both may be omitted. On the other hand, some people would add a star anise to the mixture. The addition of oil will also dilute the chillies by about half.

MAKES ABOUT 10 TABLESPOONS

12 dried red chillies
2 Thai shallots, chopped
2 garlic cloves, chopped
2 teaspoons chopped fresh galangal
1 tablespoon chopped coriander root or plant
1 tablespoon chopped lemon grass stalk and bulb

2 teaspoons chopped fresh root ginger
10 black peppercorns
¼ teaspoon coriander seeds
¼ teaspoon cumin seeds
¼ teaspoon ground cinnamon
1 teaspoon ground turmeric
6 tablespoons vegetable oil
salt

Soak the chillies in warm water until soft, drain and then seed them, if you like, before chopping them roughly. Lightly pound or process together the chillies, shallots, garlic, galangal, coriander root, lemon grass and ginger, and then add the peppercorns and spices. Continue until smooth and gradually add the vegetable oil and salt to taste. Store in a well-sealed jar in the refrigerator.

RED CURRY PASTE 2

This Thai House recipe will be marginally less hot but noticeably more fragrant, partly because of the ingredients included, partly because it is not diluted with oil.

MAKES ABOUT 15 TABLESPOONS

12 dried red chillies
3 tablespoons chopped Thai shallots
4 tablespoons chopped garlic
1 tablespoon chopped fresh galangal
2 tablespoons chopped lemon grass
stalk and bulb
2 tablespoons chopped kaffir lime zest
1 tablespoon chopped coriander
root or plant

2 teaspoons white peppercorns
1½ teaspoons cumin seeds, roasted
and ground
2 tablespoons kapi (shrimp paste)
2 teaspoons salt
2 pieces of star anise (ie, 2 'points' of
a 'star')

Prepare the chillies as above and seed them. Pound or process everything together. Store in a well-sealed jar in the refrigerator.

A tablespoon of roasted and ground coriander seeds might also be added. You can also make a green curry paste using this recipe, adding about 1½ teaspoons of fresh turmeric and using up to 80 small fresh green chillies rather than dried red ones.

Dried shrimps: Exactly what they seem to be. The best are very much the colour you would expect cooked shrimp to be, for they have been boiled and shelled before drying – a nice pinky orange with patches of white is about right. They are salty, and particularly used to add a savoury base to curry pastes, often in combination with *kapi* (shrimp paste). They can also be fried or just pounded to use as a garnish.

Fish sauce: See *nam pla*.

Galangal: Often called lesser ginger, sometimes Siamese ginger, this related root is certainly less hot but is very much more fragrant, with a hint of camphor to the flavour. It is that which gives it such affinity with the citric lemon grass and kaffir lime leaves; ordinary ginger can taste medicinal when combined with them and is not a recommended alternative.

Although galangal is available dried, the flavour seems quite different to me and I would rather do without or use ginger and go easy on anything citric.

Garlic: The typical small cloves of Thai garlic, with their thin skins, are often pounded into pastes whole. Peeling them would take hours. Larger-cloved Western garlic should always be relieved of its coarser skins. Unusually, Thai cooks generally gild garlic in oil, both as the base of a dish and as a lavish garnish. Provided you brown the garlic gently and slowly, without a hint of carbonizing, you are rewarded with something crisp and sweet, quite the reverse of what we have always been warned. It's quite a surprise, quickly addictive and adaptable to almost every other type of cuisine. Rules *are* made to be broken.

Kaffir limes: These remarkably ugly members of the lime family have the sweetest and most intense of lime flavourings. They have little or no useful juice, and so it is the fresh leaf or the grated zest that is used. Like lemon grass, the leaf can be used as a flavouring; it is infused in dishes, roughly torn into big pieces, and not eaten. The most common and effective use is to stir it into a hot dish just before serving, which intensifies the flavour. Otherwise, remove the central ribs from each leaf, roll the pieces tightly and slice them very finely, in which case, eat the leaf.

The leaves of other citrus trees can be used but will not have precisely the same flavour. Kaffir lime leaf is remarkable in its affinities and well worth the attention of an experimental cook; I use it instead of mint under the skin of lamb or duck, for instance.

The grated or chopped zest of kaffir limes is mainly used in curry pastes; as with other citrus it is very important to use only the coloured portion of the skin and as little as possible of the white, which is particularly bitter. The more common West Indian lime is a good substitute, without quite reaching the same culinary heights.

Frankly, I don't think the dried leaves or zest are worth using. Freezing will change and darken the colour of both and soften the texture, making them easier to use in making curry pastes but less attractive as a garnish.

(OVERLEAF): *Useful storecupboard ingredients*

Rice noodles

Rice noodles

Coconut milk

Cumin seeds

Palm sugar

Coriander seeds

Dried Chinese mushrooms

Mung bean noodles

Egg noodles

Nam pla – fish sauce

Black sticky rice

Jasmine rice

White sticky rice

Light soy sauce

Dried shrimp

Kapi – shrimp paste

Tamarind paste

Dark soy sauce

Red curry paste

Dried chillies

Dried chillies

Green curry paste

Sweet chilli dipping sauce

Kapi (shrimp paste): Invasive and to some nauseating, this paste of fermented and dried shrimps nevertheless becomes quite addictive. The paler the colour, the higher the quality and the more freshly made it is likely to be, although some very good versions appear rather purplish because of the black eyes of a particular type of shrimp used. In broad terms, the paler one is best for curry pastes, the darker one for *nam prik* (pages 65–7).When shrimp paste is roasted before use, it needs a wrapping of banana leaf or cooking foil; toast it under a slow grill until inspection reveals it has evenly darkened in colour. Oven gloves or great dexterity with tongs are a prerequisite of the technique.

Krachai: This is wild or white ginger and has a fascinating delicate flavour, rather citric at first but perfumed enough to be confused with galangal. It is rarely used, but essential to the making of *Kapi* balls, one of the most essential accompaniments to *Khao Chae*, the complicated dish we shared as part of a Royal Banquet.

Lemon grass: This is indeed a grass, with a warm, sweet flavour, rather like that of lemon balm. There are two main parts used, and they are used in two ways. For background flavour, the woody stems are sliced thinly at an acute angle, in big enough pieces so diners know they are not meant to be eaten; in curry pastes, the softer and more fragrant bases will also be included.

When lemon grass finishes a dish or is used as a garnish, only the juicier bulb is used, sliced very thinly indeed. Like lime leaf, lemon grass repays exploration; it makes a terrific salad when strewn over ripe tomatoes, for instance.

Nam pla (fish sauce): Think of this as liquid salt with added flavour and you'll be OK. Because it is actually made by fermenting whole small fish, in the way Romans made *garum*, some find the thought overwhelms the palate and can't bear to use it. Frankly, Worcestershire sauce is made in somewhat the same way. The really squeamish can use anchovy sauce or just salt. But it won't be the same.

Noodles: Rice noodles have the very distinct advantage of needing little or no cooking, even when dried. Pour boiling or very hot water on them and they are soon rehydrated and ready to enjoy. The wetter and fresher they are when bought, the less time they will need in the water. They are made commercially in flat sheets and then cut into varying widths: vermicelli noodles are the thinnest but the precise width used in any recipe is very much a matter of individual preference. Mung-bean noodles are prepared in the same way; egg noodles are cooked until tender in boiling water.

Palm sugar: The crystallized and slightly caramelized natural syrup or sap of a number of palms, which these days includes the coconut palm. It has two particular attributes, apart from its sweetness, both of which come directly from the caramelizing effect of applying heat to encourage the crystallizing. Firstly, this adds a wonderful richness and complexity of flavour and then it gives a complete spectrum of taste, from sweet to sharp and bitter. Thus, palm sugar adds great depth to a dish and much greater gratification than white sugar, which is one-dimensional. Although brown sugars are often recommended as a substitute, none makes such a contribution to both sweet and savoury dishes; white sugar is occasionally given as an alternative here, in recipes where the acidity of palm sugar is not needed.

Once you have opened the pack, store it in the refrigerator or freezer; it is very hygroscopic and becomes liquid if left at room temperature and then it has a tendency to ferment. If you have the misfortune to buy palm sugar that has, unusually, turned rock solid, cover it with a damp tea towel and leave it overnight; or put the lump over low heat with a sprinkle of water, adding more from time to time and stirring occasionally, until you get a thick paste.

Pomelo: These large members of the citrus family taste rather like grapefruit but have the peculiar attribute of being easily separated into the individual 'tears' which make up each segment. The effect is like crunchy crab flakes which is useful as a fascinating garnish as well, of course, as an ingredient in Thai salads of many kinds.

Rices: The white rice to use is jasmine or fragrant rice, now much more widely available, even in commercial brands. It is best cooked by the absorption method, which preserves as much flavour as possible, or by steaming, which takes a very long time. Note that this type of rice does not absorb as much water as other long-grain rices; to each measure of dry rice, use only 1 to 1¼ measures of water or stock.

One decent-sized cup of rice makes a Western main course serving for two people and, in a microwave, will cook as though steamed in 6–8 minutes on high (in an 850-watt oven). Let it stand for 5 minutes before stirring and serving. Two cups of rice will cook in 10–12 minutes.

Sticky or glutinous rice is the one preferred in the north of Thailand.

The only way to cook this is by first soaking it overnight or in hot water for 3 hours or so, and then steaming it. This is best done by wrapping the rice in thin muslin and putting it into a steamer or colander over boiling water. It always seems to take about 30 minutes, regardless of quantity. Sticky rice is eaten by rolling it into small balls in your hand and dipping it into dishes which are themselves eaten with spoon and fork.

Black sticky rice is often served as part of a dessert but the white sticky rice is specially enjoyed with green or ripe mangoes, with or without a topping of coconut cream.

Shallots, Thai: Throughout the book, I have specified 'Thai shallots', by which I mean the small purple shallot commonly found in Thailand, which, in common with all shallots, has a sweeter, lighter and more fragrant flavour than onion. I think it's worth seeking out the proper article, which is easily available from oriental food shops but, if you can't get them, the best alternatives are either brown-skinned European shallots or sweet, red-fleshed onions. Either of these is preferable to brown-skinned onions. If, however, you must use onions, use fewer and perhaps blanch them in boiling water for a few minutes before using, to reduce their acidity.

The lingering flavour and acidity even of Thai shallots has been considered in the preparation of traditional meals; in a three-course Western meal they will appear far more potent and aggressive, at the same time interacting adversely with wine in a way which Thai cooks could never conceive. It is best to serve beer if you must have plenty of shallot or onion.

Shrimp paste: See *kapi*.

Soy sauce: Not commonly used in Thai cooking but the only substitute for *nam pla* (fish sauce) if you are entertaining vegetarians. The light one is most generally used to add a salty piquancy; the darker, sweeter version is mainly used to give colour where it is needed.

Tamarind: The dried pods and seeds of the tamarind tree are soaked in hot water to give an astringent liquid which acts like lemon juice, giving fruity acidity. Soak a good tablespoon of the pulp in 300 ml (10 fl oz) of very hot water for 10 minutes. Squeeze the pulp and then strain off the tamarind water, which is the only part used. Make more or less in proportion, but it will keep refrigerated if stored in a tightly closed bottle or jar.

Turmeric: The thin brightly orange roots of fresh turmeric give a sharp, scented flavour that has nothing to do with the wet-cardboard of the dried variety. Although mostly associated with the cookery of northern Thailand, it is included in flavouring pastes all over the country. The dried powder is not an alternative as both the flavour and colour are too far removed from that of the fresh roots.

STREET FOOD AND APPETIZERS

The seemingly strange conjunction in this chapter title is intended. What you might buy as a snack or one-dish meal from a street stall in Thailand is often also perfect to begin a Western meal or to serve with drinks. That's true of dishes in other chapters, too. Don't be rigid when you are eating Thai-style but mix and match recipes from throughout the book, remembering only to keep in mind the ideal of as much contrast of flavour and texture as possible.

PORK AND PRAWN DIP
Khao Tung Na Tung

This is something to serve with drinks, with crisp rice crackers, Melba toast or plain crackers, as a nice contrast amidst such other snacks as poached and shelled quail's eggs or crudités. You can use just pork, or just prawns, of course.

SERVES 8

100 g (4 oz) raw, shelled prawns,
finely chopped
100 g (4 oz) lean minced pork
600 ml (1 pint) coconut milk
2 tablespoons chopped coriander
plant, including root
2 tablespoons chopped garlic
100 g (4 oz) Thai shallots, chopped
2 teaspoons tomato purée

4 tablespoons roasted peanuts,
roughly chopped
3 tablespoons nam pla (fish sauce)
2 tablespoons palm sugar

TO GARNISH
sliced fresh coriander leaves
fresh red chillies, cut in julienne
strips

Combine the prawns, pork, coconut milk, coriander and garlic in a saucepan and bring to the boil, stirring. Cook for a few minutes until the pork is thoroughly cooked. Once the prawns and pork are cooked, add the shallots and tomato purée and continue cooking gently until the shallots are tender. Now add the peanuts, *nam pla* and sugar and bring the mixture to a full, rolling boil. Pour it into a suitable bowl and garnish with the coriander and chillies.

FISH CAKES
Tod Mun Pla

Once you know to expect these to be rather rubbery and achieve such a texture, you will have the real thing. Make them large or small, according to whether they are to be finger food or served at table The best results are often achieved with a mixture of, say, cod and coley or other white fish.

The simple dipping sauce of vinegar and chillies, tempered with palm sugar and lime juice, is a popular accompaniment. It's just as nice, and much simpler, to offer a commercial sweet chilli sauce and fresh lime segments.

Spring onions can replace the green beans and, together with the usual condiments and the pickled cucumber suggested here, you might serve a salad of sliced cucumber in a little white vinegar, sweetened lightly with sugar and spiked with a little sliced chilli.

MAKES 6–12 FISH CAKES

1 kg (2¼ lb) boneless, skinless white fish
2 tablespoons red or green curry paste (pages 14–16)
4 tablespoons plain flour
4 tablespoons cornflour
4 eggs
6 tablespoons nam pla *(fish sauce)*

2 tablespoons palm or white sugar
about 250 ml (8 fl oz) water
100 g (4 oz) green beans, finely sliced
vegetable oil, for frying

TO SERVE
pickled cucumber

Use a processor to make a paste of the fish. Then add the curry paste, flours, eggs, *nam pla* and sugar. Slowly add water until you have a thick, sticky paste that holds its shape; you might need more or less, depending on the state of your flour. Fold in the green beans.

Form into small or large patties and either deep-fry or shallow-fry until golden brown; drain and serve with pickled cucumber.

(OVERLEAF, FROM LEFT): *Fish Cakes, Satay Sticks and Chom's Tongsai Bay Curried Mussels*

MUSSEL FRITTERS
Hoi Tod

Oysters or prawns can also be cooked like this; small European mussels are better than the large, green-lipped type, because they do not have to be cut up. Use more or less mussels or other seafood, according to whether they will be a snack or appetizer or the basis of a light meal. Serving a Thai sweet chilli sauce, plus the usual condiments, means each diner can make each fritter seem quite different.

MAKES 4 FRITTERS

FOR THE FRITTERS
8 tablespoons plain flour
4 tablespoons cornflour
about 250 ml (8 fl oz) water or fish stock
4 tablespoons nam pla (fish sauce)
6–12 or more mussels, according to size

vegetable oil, for frying (optional)

TO SERVE:
4 eggs
4 small handfuls of bean sprouts
4 tablespoons fresh coriander leaves
white pepper
Thai sweet chilli sauce

Mix together the flours and whisk in just enough of the water or stock to make a thick frying batter. Stir in the nam pla and then the mussels.

Make the fritters one at a time. Heat the oil, if using (you can do this without oil in a non-stick pan) or the pan, if not. Take an even-handed portion of the batter and mussels and fry it until the bottom is browned. Crack an egg on to it and stir the outer edges of the white lightly, breaking up the fritter slightly and allowing the whites to dribble in, as you would when cooking an omelette. Reshape the fritter as you do, making it smaller and thicker, so there is room to fry a handful of bean sprouts in the pan. When the reshaped fritter is set (the yolk will still be quite runny), turn it over and brown the other side. As it is browning, move it to one side, put in the bean sprouts, according to your enjoyment of these, and heat them through.

Put the hot sprouts on to a plate first and then put the mussel fritter on top of them. Garnish with coriander leaves and season with white pepper to taste. Serve with a Thai sweet chilli sauce, plus the usual condiments.

CHOM'S TONGSAI BAY CURRIED OYSTERS OR MUSSELS
Ho-Mok Hoi Nang-Rom

Flattish-shelled, native British oysters are too delicately flavoured to be served like this but most other varieties make a succulent first course that is easily multiplied for more people.

It's much cheaper and just as traditional to use mussels; the ready-cooked New Zealand, green-shelled mussels would be best. One of those is equivalent to an oyster as far as this recipe is concerned.

For spectacular presentation, set the prepared oysters on an ovenproof dish covered with a thick layer of sea-salt flakes and then grill or bake them.

SERVES 6

6 fresh oysters or large mussels on the half shell
8 tablespoons coconut cream
2 teaspoons red curry paste (pages 15–16)
1 teaspoon very finely sliced kaffir lime leaves

1 large egg
1 teaspoon nam pla (fish sauce)
1 large fresh red chilli, finely sliced
12 fresh coriander leaves

TO GARNISH
24 fresh basil leaves

Take the oysters from their shells and blanch them in boiling water for 30 seconds only, just to set the flesh. Mix together the coconut cream, curry paste, lime leaves, egg and *nam pla*. Fold in the oysters and then spoon each back into its shell, with the sauce. Decorate with the chilli and coriander leaves.

Steam over boiling water for about 5 minutes or until heated through and lightly set. These would microwave in about 90 seconds, more or less, on high (in an 850-watt oven); start with a minute and check.

Serve whilst still hot, sprinkled with the basil leaves.

LETTUCE LEAVES WITH THAI ACCOMPANIMENTS
Meang Kum

The braver and more creative you are, the more brilliant and memorable this display platter can be. Ask in Thai shops to be shown the other leaves they might eat with *meang* (sometimes *mieng*) and follow their lead: the pointed leaf which comes in ribbed spades, *cha plu*, is especially popular. But every one of the styles of filling or sauce is also delicious with lettuce and certainly enjoyed like that in Thailand, too. This first recipe is from the supremely elegant Thai restaurant of Bangkok's Beaufort Sukhothai Hotel; it's followed by simpler ones. This is wonderful buffet and party food, of course. Cooks with plenty of time actually make these up for their guests: an opportunity for a stunning arrangement and centrepiece.

SERVES 6

FOR THE SAUCE
1 tablespoon kapi (*shrimp paste*)
½ tablespoon *sliced fresh galangal*
½ tablespoon *sliced Thai shallot*
2 tablespoons *desiccated coconut*
3 tablespoons *chopped dry-roasted peanuts*
2 tablespoons *chopped dried shrimps*
1 teaspoon *peeled and thinly sliced fresh root ginger*
175–225 g (6–8 oz) *palm sugar*
600 ml (1 pint) *coconut milk or water*

lightly browned
3 tablespoons *finely chopped Thai shallots*
3 tablespoons *finely chopped whole-limes*
3 tablespoons *finely chopped fresh root ginger*
3 tablespoons *small dried shrimps, chopped*
3 tablespoons *dry-roasted peanuts*
2 tablespoons *chopped small green chillies*

FOR THE ACCOMPANIMENTS
6 tablespoons *desiccated coconut,*

TO SERVE
lettuce leaves

Roast the *kapi* in the usual way (see page 20), together with the galangal and shallots, and then leave to cool. Pound or process these ingredients with the coconut, peanuts, dried shrimps and ginger. Mix in the sugar and water or coconut milk, and then simmer until it has reduced to about 300 m (10 fl oz) of thickish coating sauce.

Put the sauce into a serving bowl and surround it with the remaining ingredients. To eat, fill individual lettuce or other leaves with a mixture of the accompaniments, top them with the sauce, roll and enjoy, making the combination and flavour treats different every time.

CHICKEN MEANG
Fry a tablespoon each of finely chopped coriander root or plant and garlic with their combined volume of green peppercorns until a light golden brown. Stir in 225 g (8 oz) of finely chopped chicken breast and, when that is cooked, flavour with 2 tablespoons of light soy sauce and 1 table-spoon of palm sugar. Cook gently until almost all the liquid is absorbed. Taste, perhaps adding more soy sauce because the saltiness should dominate the sweetness. Serve as above, with the same sort of accompaniments; cashews can be substituted for peanuts.

SMOKED FISH MEANG
This time, the dipping sauce is simply a mixture of 3 tablespoons of *nam pla*, 1 tablespoon of palm sugar, 2 teaspoons of lime or lemon juice, a chopped chilli or two and just enough water to make it spoonable. The accompaniments include about 175 g (6 oz) of lightly flaked smoked fish and, perhaps, a slightly higher quantity of chopped lime or lemon flesh and, if you do it the authentic way, masses of whole small garlic cloves.

GALLOPING HORSES
Ma Ho

No, I can't find out why this delicious snack is called what it is. However, as well as pineapple, make it with *longans* (rather like lychees) or peeled orange slices; in fact, you could pick anything fruity and tropical, I expect.

This is a tastier and simpler version of a dish I found in Chiang Mai which included pickled turnip rather than coriander and black peppercorns. As that is a little difficult to buy, I thought you'd appreciate this version.

Do take the time to ensure that the mixture is a really rich colour before serving it.

MAKES AT LEAST 18

3 tablespoons vegetable oil
2 tablespoons finely chopped garlic
1 tablespoon finely chopped coriander
root or plant
5 black peppercorns
1 teaspoon salt
225 g (8 oz) minced pork
4 tablespoons (or more to taste) dry-
roasted peanuts, chopped
2 tablespoons white or palm sugar
2 tablespoons nam pla (fish sauce)

TO SERVE
fresh pineapple wedges, orange slices,
longans, or a mixture, peeled as
necessary and cut in bite-size
pieces

TO GARNISH
fresh coriander leaves

Heat the oil and then stir-fry the garlic, coriander, peppercorns and salt until nicely fragrant. Then add the pork and peanuts and continue cooking until the pork is cooked through. Add the sugar and the *nam pla* and then cook until the ingredients have thickened and are a good caramel colour; add more sugar or *nam pla*, if you like, to make a sweet/salt flavour and a slightly sticky texture. Leave to cool.

Arrange the prepared fruit on a platter, perhaps lined with an oiled banana leaf, cut to shape. Top each with some of the prepared mixture and then garnish with the coriander leaves.

SATAY STICKS

A tremendous street-snack favourite at any time of the day; it is even common to see schoolchildren scurrying with these in the mornings. Satay sticks (Thais sometimes use the spelling *satei*) can be served just with the usual Thai condiments but are much more enjoyable with a peanut sauce. My quick version can be the basis for your own experiments, noting that it does not need to include chillies. Satays are so popular that you can easily double the recipe and still end up with empty plates; thus, the number of servings made with this recipe is entirely arbitrary. If you have no red curry paste to hand, you might use only turmeric powder, palm sugar, salt and vinegar as we saw in Bangkok's Chinatown, or an Indian curry paste. Or almost anything.

SERVES 4

450 g (1 lb) lean pork, chicken or beef

FOR THE MARINADE
8–10 tablespoons coconut milk
up to 1 tablespoon red curry paste (pages 15–16)
1 tablespoon nam pla (fish sauce)
1–2 teaspoons palm sugar

FOR THE SAUCE
4 heaped tablespoons crunchy peanut butter
150 ml (5 fl oz) coconut cream
1 garlic clove, chopped
1 tablespoon palm sugar
2 tablespoons nam pla (fish sauce)
chilli paste, or fresh chillies, cut in julienne strips
finely sliced lemon grass bulb or kaffir lime leaf

The meat should be trimmed of all fat and then thinly sliced, to a maximum width and length of 20 x 2.5 cm (8 x 1 inch). Combine the marinade ingredients and toss the meat evenly in the marinade. Let it marinate for 1 hour at room temperature or 4 in a refrigerator (longer is better). Meanwhile, soak wooden skewers in water for several hours.

Weave each strip onto a stick: if you make narrow ones you can put two on to each stick, perhaps mixing chicken and pork, for instance. Grill or barbecue over medium heat until cooked through; alternatively, do not thread them on sticks but stir-fry them in a non-stick pan.

To make the sauce, combine all the ingredients and bring to a gentle boil. When well blended, pour into a bowl and serve hot, with the freshly cooked satay sticks.

PRAWN AND COCONUT OMELETTE
Khanom Buang Kai

This is a terrific way to convert people to the fascinating flavours of Thailand, with not a chilli in sight (although it should be served with the usual challenging condiments). The dish makes a very nice lunch or light supper for two people and a gratifyingly magnificent feast for one.

SERVES 2–4

4 tablespoons vegetable oil
1 tablespoon chopped garlic
225–275 g (8–10 oz) raw, shelled prawns, roughly chopped
3 tablespoons desiccated coconut
25–50 g (1–2 oz) bean sprouts
1–2 tablespoons nam pla (fish sauce)
1–2 tablespoons palm sugar

FOR THE OMELETTE:
3 eggs
½ teaspoon salt
4 tablespoons stock or water

TO GARNISH
fresh coriander leaves

Heat the oil and stir-fry the garlic until a light golden brown and then add the prawns and cook until they're almost done. Add the coconut and bean sprouts and toss until they're heated through. Flavour with *nam pla* and sugar; a little sweetness is always a help with fish and seafood, so don't stint on the sugar. If you are using ready-cooked prawns, add them last and just heat them through.

Lightly whisk together the eggs, salt and stock or water and then cook in a non-stick pan, big enough to give a thin, crêpe-like result, rather than anything like a pancake or thick omelette. Do not turn but, once it is set, pile the prepared stuffing into the centre and then fold in the sides to make a rectangular package. Turn out neatly, with the folds underneath, and garnish with coriander leaves.

SOUPS

A soup is essential to an authentic Thai dinner. Sipped and supped throughout the meal rather than as a first course, soups offer soothing textural contrast to drier dishes and also help keep up liquid intake in the country's hot climate. On other occasions, soups make a light, homely lunch or supper or introduce a modern Western meal that might start with Thai flavours and move on to some other part of the world. Essentially, there are just two main styles. The *kaeng chud* are based on clear liquids or stocks and clearly inspired by China; the *tom yum* family is thick and rich with coconut milk and cream. Of course, though not in this chapter, soups are also served with noodles, when they become a one-dish meal to be enjoyed at any time of the day, out and about or at home.

CHIVA-SOM VEGETABLE STOCK

This is what you need for the *Cucumber and Egg Soup* (page 38). You could, of course, use something more citric for the stock, such as the base of the *Mussels in a Lemon Grass Broth* recipe (page 37), but here is what Chef Andrew Jacka, executive chef of the Chiva-Som Health Resort, serves.

MAKES ABOUT 2 LITRES (3½ PINTS)

8 very ripe tomatoes, chopped
1 small Chinese cabbage, shredded
4 Chinese celery stalks, or celery
leaves and thin stalks, chopped

4 carrots, chopped
4 litres (6½ pints) water

Combine all the ingredients in a large pan, bring to the boil and then simmer for 1 hour, lightly covered. It should reduce by about half.
    Strain through muslin and then discard the vegetables. Season to taste, perhaps reducing further according to the purposes to which you may put it.

STUFFED MUSHROOM SOUP
Kaeng Chud Hed Yud Sai

This soup and the next one are clearly influenced by China and make a welcome contrast to other dishes, for they never contain coconut and quite often have no chilli either. I know that Superwoman Shirley Conran reckons life is too short to stuff mushrooms but, clearly, she had never tasted these ones. This is pretty much Charmaine Solomon's recipe, always a good start.

Cheats could simply poach the stuffed mushrooms in my *Lemon Grass Broth* (page 37) or any other stock which appeals, as long as it is thin, as clear as possible, and utterly fat free.

For particularly elegant occasions and when you happen to have a crystal-clear clarified stock, the stuffed mushrooms should be steamed or microwaved separately; for when they are cooked in the stock there will inevitably be some clouding. If you can get it and like it, bitter (winter) melon is more traditional than cucumber.

SERVES 4–6

12 dried shiitake mushrooms
100 g (4 oz) minced pork or raw, shelled prawns
1 teaspoon finely chopped garlic
2–3 spring onions, finely chopped
1 tablespoon chopped fresh coriander root or plant
1 tablespoon light soy sauce
ground white pepper
2–3 canned water chestnuts, drained
1.2 litres (2 pints) clear chicken or vegetable stock
36 cucumber arcs (page 56)
nam pla (fish sauce)
fresh chillies, cut in julienne strips

Soak the mushrooms in very hot water for 30 minutes and then squeeze them gently. Cut off the stems and use them for extra flavour in the stock if you like, but don't actually serve them.

Choose pork, prawns or a mixture of both and gently combine your choice with the garlic, half the spring onions, the coriander, soy sauce, white pepper to taste and water chestnuts. Stuff the mushroom caps evenly with this mixture and then poach for 15–20 minutes in just enough of the chicken stock to cover (more than this will encourage the mushrooms to float and lose their filling before it is cooked).

When ready to serve, remove the hot mushrooms and serve two per person. Add the remaining stock to the saucepan, bring to the boil and add the cucumber arcs and *nam pla* to taste. Simmer for a couple of minutes, until the cucumber begins to look a little transparent. Ladle the soup and hot cucumber carefully into the soup plates and sprinkle the remaining spring onion and a few chilli slices on top, if you like or dare.

MUSSELS IN A LEMON GRASS BROTH

I created this as a simple introduction to the ease of cooking Thai-style for, as you see, there are plenty of choices to make if some ingredients are hard to come by in your area.

Serve this as a first course or as a light main course, Western style: in a Thai meal it makes the ideal soup accompaniment but you might want to halve the quantity. Greenshell mussels from New Zealand are usually bought pre-cooked: if you start with uncooked mussels, you'll need to cook them for a little longer, but not much.

SERVES 4–6

6 large lemon grass stalks
100 g (4 oz) Thai shallots, quartered
4 garlic cloves, crushed
50 g (2 oz) fresh galangal, or fresh root ginger, peeled and sliced
2 limes, quartered, or 4 kaffir lime leaves, torn
2 small fresh red chillies, seeded and chopped, or Tabasco sauce

1 teaspoon salt, 1 teaspoon black peppercorns
1.2 litres (2 pints) cold water
1 kg (2¼ lb) New Zealand greenshell mussels on the half shell

TO GARNISH
fresh coriander leaves

Crush and slice four of the lemon grass stalks and put them into a large casserole with the shallots, garlic, galangal or ginger, limes or lime leaves, chillies or Tabasco sauce to taste, salt and peppercorns. Add the water and bring very slowly to the boil. Leave to simmer for 15 minutes and then let it stand, covered and off the heat, until cool.

Strain the infusion and return to the casserole. Cut off and crush the bulb end only of the remaining lemon grass stalks and slice these very thinly. Bring back to the boil and then add the mussels and let them heat through without boiling again. If using fresh mussels, simmer them just until the shells are opened. Garnish with fresh coriander, of course.

BABY CORN AND BASIL SOUP
Kaeng Liang Ruam Phak

Such other sweet vegetables as pumpkin or fresh green peas and beans might also be cooked in this light, chilli-free soup. It's very refreshing to the palate when served with strong-tasting food and was part of the menu made for us at The Thai House.

SERVES 4–6

10 whole white peppercorns	1.2 litres (2 pints) stock or water
1 tablespoon kapi (shrimp paste), roasted	450 g (1 lb) baby corn cobs
10 Thai shallots, chopped	30–40 fresh basil leaves
4 tablespoons dried shrimps	2–3 tablespoons nam pla (fish sauce)

Pound or process together the peppercorns, *kapi*, shallots and dried shrimps until you have an even paste. Mix the paste and stock together in a saucepan. Bring to the boil, uncovered, stirring constantly.

Slice the baby corn cobs diagonally, lengthways. Add the corn and basil to the mixture in the pan. Bring to the boil, and simmer until the corn is tender (just a few minutes). Season with *nam pla* and serve at once.

CUCUMBER AND EGG SOUP

An unusual recipe from Chiva-Som, Thailand's first health resort. Although it seems Western, it was developed by the resort's Thai chefs, using a stock recipe from the sous chef's mother, and is specially suited to being served as a first course, Western style. If you are serving vegetarians, remember to replace the *nam pla* with soy sauce.

SERVES 6

1.2 litres (2 pints) cold Chiva-Som Vegetable Stock (page 35)	6 spring onions, thinly sliced
350 g (12 oz) cucumber, peeled, halved lengthways, seeded and thickly sliced	4–6 tablespoons nam pla (fish sauce)
	white pepper
	3 egg whites

Put the cold stock and prepared cucumber into a saucepan and bring to the boil. Add the spring onions and leave to simmer for 5 minutes, being certain you do not let the onions lose their bright colour. Stir in *nam pla* to taste and then season with white pepper to taste. Bring to the boil.

Lightly beat the egg whites, whisk them into the boiling soup where they will make fine threads, and then serve immediately.

CHICKEN GALANGAL SOUP
Kai Tom Kha

One of the two greatest Thai soups, coconut-creamy and more fragrant than the better known *Tom Yum Goong* (page 41). This first version is from The Thai House and is simple and rustic without surrendering any of the essential appeal.

SERVES 4–6

1 litre (1¾ pints) coconut milk
450 g (1 lb) boneless, skinless chicken breast, sliced
bulbs of 2 lemon grass stalks, finely sliced
50 g (2 oz) fresh galangal, finely sliced
5 kaffir lime leaves, finely shredded

3 tablespoons nam pla *(fish sauce)*
225 g (8 oz) straw mushrooms, halved
150 ml (5 fl oz) coconut cream
5 tablespoons lime juice
up to 5 hot fresh chillies, chopped
2–3 fresh coriander plants, including roots, chopped

Pour the coconut milk into a large saucepan and then add the chicken, lemon grass, galangal and lime leaves. Bring slowly to the boil, by which time the chicken should be cooked. Stir in the *nam pla* and then the straw mushrooms and the coconut cream. Return to the boil, stirring all the time.

Mix in the lime juice, chillies and coriander and then serve at once.

THE ORIENTAL HOTEL'S CHICKEN GALANGAL SOUP
Kai Tom Kha Oriental

Chef Vitchit of The Oriental makes a rather more complicated version of this famed soup, which repays the little extra effort with a much richer, more sophisticated flavour.

SERVES 4–6

7 large garlic cloves, peeled
3 whole white peppercorns
7 coriander roots, or 2–3 complete plants, chopped
2 lemon grass stalks, finely sliced
3 Thai shallots, chopped
100 g (4 oz) fresh galangal, finely sliced

1 litre (2 pints) coconut milk
450 g (1 lb) boneless, skinless chicken, sliced
4 tablespoons nam pla (fish sauce)
5 small hot fresh chillies, chopped
4 tablespoons lime juice
7 kaffir lime leaves, shredded
3 fresh coriander sprigs, chopped

Pound together or process the garlic, peppercorns, coriander roots or plants, lemon grass, shallots and half the galangal until you have a thick paste.

Bring a quarter of the coconut milk to the boil, stir in the galangal paste and then the chicken, stirring constantly. Add the remaining galangal and coconut milk. Bring to the boil, reduce the heat to a simmer for 15 minutes or more and leave until the chicken is tender.

Stir in the *nam pla*, chillies and lime juice and then adjust the flavourings to your taste.

Sprinkle with the lime leaves and coriander before serving. Chef Vitchit serves the soup in young coconuts: a wonderful presentation.

SOUR AND SPICY PRAWN SOUP
Tom Yam Goong

This seems to be where many people's knowledge of Thai food begins – and ends. It does not need to be fiery hot. If it is, you probably miss the point of the complicated combination of flavours, each separately identifiable, which is the sign of great Thai cuisine.

This is the version we found at The Thai House and, surprisingly, it is more complicated and more elegant than the one demonstrated at the palace – the background flavourings are strained out, for instance. An even richer colour and flavour is often appreciated, in which case, also stir a few teaspoons of red curry paste (pages 15–16) to the stock, before you add the prawns.

SERVES 4–6

2 large lemon grass stalks	200 g (7 oz) small mushrooms,
1 litre (1¾ pints) water	halved
5 thick slices of fresh galangal	4 tablespoons nam pla (fish sauce)
3 Thai shallots, chopped	4 tablespoons lime juice
4 kaffir lime leaves, torn	4 hot fresh chillies, chopped
350 g (12 oz) raw prawns, shelled	4 tablespoons or so chopped fresh
and de-veined	coriander plants, including roots

Finely slice the fleshy bulb of the lemon grass stalks and reserve: use 4–6 if they are small. Cut the remaining part of each stalk into 2.5 cm (1 inch) lengths.

Bring the water to the boil and then stir in the lengths of lemon grass, the galangal, shallots and lime leaves. Return to the boil and then remove from the heat. Leave to stand, covered, for 5 minutes. Strain and then reserve the liquid.

To continue, bring the reserved liquid to the boil and then stir in the prawns, mushrooms and *nam pla*. Simmer until the prawns are just cooked.

Stir in the lime juice, chillies, coriander and sliced lemon grass; mix well. Serve hot. On special – or royal – occasions, also buy one or two really big tiger prawns, with shells, for each serving and add them as a sensational garnish.

PUMPKIN AND COCONUT SOUP
Kaeng Liang Fak Thong

Traditionally considered the perfect nourishment for children and nursing mothers, this soup is well known in Thailand but rare outside it. The correct basil for this is *manglak*. You might find this called lemon basil – it's paler and a little more furred than common basil – but whatever you can get will do.

SERVES 4–6

450 g (1 lb) ripe pumpkin flesh, with skin, de-seeded
1 generous tablespoon lime juice
6 tablespoons dried shrimps
2 tablespoons Thai shallots, sliced
2 teaspoons kapi (shrimp paste)
2–3 fresh red chillies, chopped

1 teaspoon white peppercorns
600 ml (1 pint) thin coconut milk
300 ml (10 fl oz) thick coconut milk or cream
nam pla (fish sauce) or salt
20 fresh basil leaves

Cut the pumpkin into irregular shapes, each with some skin attached. Peel away most of the skin, leaving a thin strip across each piece: this will help keep its shape during cooking. Sprinkle with the lime juice.

Soak the dried shrimps in hot water for about 5 minutes or until softened; then drain and pound or process with the shallots, *kapi*, chillies and peppercorns, until evenly textured. Whisk into the thin coconut milk in a saucepan, bring to the boil and simmer for 5 minutes to develop the flavour. Now add the pumpkin pieces and let them cook gently. When they are tender, season with *nam pla* or salt and then stir in the thick coconut milk or cream. If the soup is too thick, it is best diluted with water or stock rather than more coconut milk.

Keep warm and, just before serving, swirl in the basil leaves and take the soup to the table immediately.

VARIATION: Charmaine Solomon, the much-respected author of *The Complete Asian Cookbook* and *The Thai Cookbook*, recommends a more complex and fragrant version, adding 8 tablespoons of tamarind water (pages 22–3) and a large finely chopped lemon grass stalk to the paste.

(OPPOSITE): *Pumpkin and Coconut Soup* (TOP) and *Royal Sour and Spicy Prawn Soup* (BELOW)

ROYAL SOUR AND SPICY PRAWN SOUP
Tom Yam Goong

Such is the national pride in the Golden Anniversary of the reign of HM King Bhumipol, that everyone wanted to help make our television series. HRH Princess Sudhasiri Sobra kindly shared this recipe when she entertained us at her small country palace. It is much simpler and lighter than many versions and, surprisingly, is thus both easier to make at home and more acceptable to novices.

All versions can be served on prepared servings of rice noodles, for a gratifying meal in a bowl. When it is also topped with creamy yellow-green prawn coral and garnished with coriander leaves it becomes *Guae Teow Tom Yum Goong*, another top favourite with yuppie business men and women.

The usual stock is a rich pork stock, flavoured only with garlic, peppercorns and Thai celery leaf, but another kind can be used, of course. As an even simpler alternative to crushing fresh chillies, ground chillies can be used, from a pinch to a teaspoon.

SERVES 4–6

about 900 ml (1½ pints) rich stock
6–12 very large raw prawns, shelled and de-veined
1 large lemon grass stalk, thinly sliced diagonally
5 or so fresh chillies, crushed (not sliced)

3 tablespoons fresh lime juice
1–2 tablespoons nam pla *(fish sauce)*
3 kaffir lime leaves, torn

Once you have brought the stock to the boil, add the lemon grass, chillies, lime juice, *nam pla* and lime leaves. Simmer for a minute and then stir in the prawns. Once they are cooked through, stir once and serve. Neither the lemon grass, nor chillies nor lime leaves are eaten. Dilute the soup with more stock, if necessary.

FRIED DISHES

The texture of a fried dish is always an important part of the complex planning of a Thai meal of more than a few dishes. Often, the ingredients might well have been steamed instead but the sensual slipperiness of oily sauces, the crispness of deep-fried foods or batters, or even the absence of any sauce can all become more important than the ingredients. Don't ignore this chapter because fried food has had bad publicity: remember these dishes are just part of a meal and only a small amount is eaten by each diner, and then not every day.

STIR-FRIED CHICKEN AND CASHEWS
Phat Himalai

The lightly cooked onion and the spring onion make this the type of robust dish favoured by those living in the harsher, colder north, as its Thai name suggests. It should be enjoyed pretty much by itself, with plain rice and vegetables, rather than being served at the same time as anything more sophisticated, for it will swamp more delicate flavours and waste your time and effort.

SERVES 4–6

2 tablespoons vegetable oil
3 garlic cloves, crushed
450 g (1 lb) boneless, skinless
chicken breast, thinly sliced
50 g (2 oz) cashew nuts, roasted
4–5 dried chillies, lightly fried

1 small onion, sliced
3 spring onions, chopped
1½ tablespoons nam pla (fish sauce)
1 tablespoon dark soy sauce
salt

Heat the oil in a large wok or pan. Add the garlic and stir-fry until a light golden brown. Add the chicken slices and stir-fry for about 5 minutes or until the chicken is cooked through but still tender and moist.

Add the cashews, chillies, onion, spring onions, *nam pla*, soy sauce and salt to taste. Stir-fry for a minute or until well mixed and heated through.

PRAWNS AND BEANS WITH CRISP-FRIED BASIL
Prikking Kai Kem

With its great colours, speed of preparation and unusual garnish, this could certainly be a main course in any Western-style meal, when it would more typically serve three or four, accompanied by rice and vegetables.

SERVES 4–6

175 g (6 oz) green beans, cut in
2.5 cm (1 inch) lengths
4 tablespoons vegetable oil
3 tablespoons red curry paste
(pages 15–16)
1½ tablespoons dried shrimps, ground
450 g (1 lb) raw prawns, shelled and
de-veined

1 tablespoon palm or white sugar
1–2 tablespoons nam pla
(fish sauce)

FOR THE CRISP-FRIED BASIL
50–60 fresh basil leaves
vegetable oil, for deep-frying

Firstly, blanch the green beans very lightly in boiling water; then drain and reserve them. Then fry the basil leaves for the garnish in deep, hot oil; drain and reserve them.

Heat the oil over a medium heat and stir-fry together the red curry paste and ground dried shrimps. When the paste is fragrant and oil is rising to the top, add the prawns and keep stirring until they are evenly cooked through; then add the beans. Once they are warmed through, flavour with the sugar and nam pla, emphasizing the sweetness of the sugar rather than saltiness. Serve at once, topped with the fried basil leaves.

ISSAN BARBECUED CHICKEN
Kai Yang

An absolute basic which can be flavoured only with the great Thai trinity – garlic, peppercorns and coriander. But because this dish seems to have originated in the north-east, where Chinese influence is identifiable, rice wine and soy sauce are often included. And because it is also eaten all over Thailand, from street stalls to palaces, you can, with impunity, allow lime juice, finely sliced lemon grass, chopped ginger or nam pla to find their way into your mixture, or include the thick coconut milk of the south. Some even leave out the coriander; this is not heresy but perfect proof that Thai food is what you want it to be. Here is a dependable framework upon which you can elaborate.

Any chilli dip will do as an accompaniment but a sweet one is best, and this boiled one seems always to go down well.

Serves 4–6

1.5 kg (3 lb) chicken pieces, with
bone

For the Marinade
1 tablespoon finely chopped garlic
2 tablespoons black peppercorns,
roughly crushed
4 tablespoons roughly chopped
coriander plants, including roots
2 tablespoons Chinese rice wine or
medium sherry
1 heaped teaspoon salt

For the Boiled Sweet
Chilli Dip
300 ml (10 fl oz) white or cider
vinegar
100 g (4 oz) palm sugar
garlic
2 or more fresh red chillies, cut in
julienne strips, or Tabasco sauce,
nam pla (fish sauce) or salt

Mix together the marinade ingredients, and then taste. Rub the mixture into the chicken and, if you can, leave them to get acquainted for at least an hour at room temperature, or for 4 hours in the refrigerator.

Grill or barbecue gently; 20–30 minutes should do it but don't use a high heat or you will carbonize the fabulous flavours. You might find it more reliable to bake the chicken in the oven at 180°C/350°F/Gas 4.

For the sweet chilli dip: boil together the vinegar and sugar with as much garlic as you fancy and the chillies. Once the dip has thickened, let it cool and then adjust the seasoning with nam pla or salt. The faint or inexperienced of palate might leave out the chillies and allow fellow diners to sprinkle on Tabasco sauce to taste.

STIR-FRIED CHICKEN WITH CHILLIES AND BASIL
Phad Kai Bai Kraprao

You will find infinite variations on this combination. Not only might the chicken be minced, sliced or cubed but the basic flavourings might be supported by soy sauce, palm sugar, peppercorns or any number of stir-fried vegetables. Here is a basic version that is very easy to halve or to multiply.

The correct basil to use is mint basil but, because this is not always possible, use the strongest tasting one you can find, or throw in a few mint leaves too. You can substitute thinly sliced pork loin for the chicken.

SERVES 2–3

*350 g (12 oz) boneless, skinless
chicken breast or thigh
2–4 fresh green chillies
2–4 large garlic cloves
1 tablespoon* nam pla *(fish sauce)*

*1–2 teaspoons palm sugar
vegetable oil, for frying
1–2 fresh red chillies, cut in
julienne strips
20–30 fresh basil leaves*

Slice the chicken finely across the grain. Pound or process together the green chillies, garlic, *nam pla* and sugar. Stir-fry the mixture in a little oil for 1 minute and then add the chicken. Continue to stir-fry until the chicken no longer looks raw and then add the chillies.

When the chicken is cooked through, mix in the basil leaves and serve at once.

THREE-FLAVOURED FISH
Pla Sam Rote

This is an example of the classic Asian technique of frying a fish until it's crisp and then pouring on to it a savoury sauce, but there's no mistaking the Thai flavours here. It's another interesting Western-style main course for two, or for many more at a Thai-style meal.

SERVES 2–4

1 whole snapper, weighing
450–750 g (1–1½ lb)
vegetable oil, for frying

FOR THE SAUCE
3 fresh red chillies
3 fresh green chilies
½ teaspoon salt
½ teaspoon sliced fresh galangal

½ teaspoon chopped coriander
root or plant
9 black or white peppercorns
2 teaspoons chopped garlic
1 tablespoon chopped Thai shallot
4 tablespoons vegetable oil
5–6 tablespoons tamarind water
(pages 22–3)
2 tablespoons palm sugar
1½ tablespoons nam pla (fish sauce)

First prepare the flavouring paste by pounding or processing together the chillies, salt, galangal, coriander, peppercorns, garlic and shallot. Fry this over medium heat in the oil until lightly golden brown and very fragrant.

Flavour with the tamarind water, sugar and *nam pla* and then cook to reduce to a sauce that is good and thick but which will still pour. The dish is named because of the equal balance of sweet, sour and salty in this sauce, so taste to ensure this is what you have achieved. Keep warm.

Score the cleaned fish deeply on both sides and then fry it in enough very hot oil to half cover it. Wait until the underside is well cooked and golden brown before turning it to cook the other side, about 5 minutes on each side depending on thickness.

Turn the fish onto a serving platter and then immediately pour on the hot sauce. A handfull of stir-fried vegetables – baby corn, red pepper, mange tout – may be added to the sauce.

DYNAMIC SEAFOOD STIR-FRY WITH LIME LEAF AND BASIL

At Tongsai Bay on Ko Samui, you can have fresh fish direct from the Gulf of Siam, golden sands, blue waters, coconut palms and Chef Chom, cooking. What more could you want? Well, fire-proofing for a start if this is what was on the menu. Of course, you can reduce the number of chillies, or leave them out altogether, using just the green peppercorns perhaps. And the more seafood with shells you include, the more the sauce becomes merely a background, very little of which is eaten. But, basically, if you like it hot, this is your stop.

Fish fillets or seafood can be used, but it looks nicer to mix prawns in their shells, some clams or mussels, scallops, squid and so on.

SERVES 2–4

450 g (1 lb) seafood
8 tablespoons vegetable oil
2–4 tablespoons nam pla
(fish sauce)
1–2 tablespoons palm or white sugar
30 fresh basil leaves
3 kaffir lime leaves, very finely
sliced

FOR THE PASTE
2 tablespoons fresh red and green
chillies, cut in julienne strips
1 tablespoon finely sliced garlic
1 tablespoon finely sliced
Thai shallot
1 tablespoon green peppercorns, fresh
or canned and drained
salt

Begin by making the paste. Pound or process together the chillies, garlic, shallot and peppercorns, with a little salt.

Stir-fry each variety of seafood by itself in plenty of very hot oil, and then set aside. Pour off half the oil and reserve the remainder in the pan.

Put the pan with the reserved oil on to medium heat and fry the paste until nicely fragrant. Quickly mix in the seafood and season with the *nam pla* and sugar. Just before serving, stir in the basil and lime leaves.

SWEET PORK
Moo Wan

Another dish to horrify health freaks – a virtual guarantee that it is delicious.
It keeps particularly well and thus makes terrific picnic food; it's much better
served cold and is also a great snack or party appetizer with long, cold drinks.
There are all sorts of ways to make it, using boiling or frying, but this combination does the job nicely. You can remove the skin first, which makes it
easier to eat and, if you are flush, skinless loin gives a grander, leaner result.
The garlic is often left out, particularly if children want to gobble this up, as
they usually do.

SERVES 4–6

450 g (1 lb) belly of pork, cut in
2.5 cm (1 inch) cubes
2 tablespoons vegetable oil
2 teaspoons chopped garlic

2 tablespoons palm sugar
1 tablespoon dark soy sauce
4 tablespoons nam pla (fish sauce)

A large, non-stick frying-pan is the best utensil in which to cook this.
Heat the oil and lightly fry the garlic, allowing it to take a little
colour, in the Thai way. Now add everything else but, if you are unsure of
these flavours, only add half the soy sauce and *nam pla* at this stage. Don't
cover the pan or fiddle with the pork by stirring it too often but sprinkle
in a spoonful of water from time to time if you think it all looks too dry
before the pork is tender.

Once an appropriate degree of succulence is reached, taste and adjust
with palm sugar or *nam pla*. You should end up with tender cubes in a
clinging, syrupy sauce. It will be concentrated enough to catch and burn
easily, hence the advantage of a non-stick pan so you can turn it, if you
must.

Belly of pork may take 35–40 minutes, but tenderloin only takes 10–12
minutes to cook through, perhaps less.

CRISP PORK BELLY
Moo Grob

There is a lot of frying to this recipe, which I found in a very old Thai book, written before fat and frying were wicked words. But as a special picnic or party dish I can't think of anything more enjoyable for so little real work. It's easy and it's cheap! Ideally, serve this with a chilli sauce spiked with lime juice and soothed with sugar.

I have seen something similar to this finished by being quickly mixed into a stir-fried mixture of chopped galangal, chillies, coriander root, *nam pla*, palm sugar and so forth. Could be good. With extra vegetables, this could become a fascinating meal of great textural contrasts.

SERVES 4–6

1 kg (2¼ lb) boned weight belly of pork, in one piece	1 large head of garlic, cloves separated but not peeled
1 tablespoon salt	4 whole coriander plants
1 tablespoon black peppercorns	2–3 tablespoons cider vinegar

I suppose you could begin with sliced belly of pork, often sold as spare ribs, but it seems more fun to do it the old way. If you have the choice, a piece of pork with thin skin will cook faster.

Put all the ingredients, except the vinegar, into a large saucepan and cover with cold water. Bring to the boil and continue boiling until the pork skin is very tender. You will need to skim regularly and expect it to take an hour, perhaps more, depending on the ratio of meat to fat; the tenderness of the skin is paramount.

Drain and, while still warm, use a knife with a very sharp point to score through the skin in straight lines about 2.5 cm (1 inch) apart and then do the same thing at right angles.

When cool, brush with the vinegar and allow to dry completely. Do this two more times. Now preheat the oven to 200°C/400°F/Gas 6 and bake the pork on a rack for 40 minutes or more until it is gorgeously golden and crisp.

You might think you can eat it now. You can't. Carve the pork cross-wise into slices, along the incisions you made, and then fry them in hot lard until they're crackling crisp. Cut these across into bite-size pieces. Now you can eat.

THAI ROASTED PORK WITH PINEAPPLE SALAD

You will probably want to cook this as a main course for a Western-style meal. But as the centrepiece of a buffet it would clearly serve many more than six. It's based on a recipe I found in *Everyday Siamese Dishes* by Sibpan Sonakul, published decades ago in Bangkok and illustrated with black and white photographs taken by HM the King. The same method would be good with chicken or duck, I imagine.

Continue the tropical theme by also serving orange-fleshed sweet potatoes, perhaps mashed with coconut milk, and a quick stir-fry of green vegetables. If you can buy only a large pineapple, use just half the flesh for this delicious salad, perhaps using the rest to make *Galloping Horses* (page 32).

SERVES 6

1 tablespoon chopped garlic	2 tablespoons dark soy sauce
1–2 tablespoons black peppercorns, roughly crushed	4 tablespoons palm or caster sugar
4 tablespoons chopped coriander plant, including roots	FOR THE SALAD
vegetable oil, if necessary	1 small fresh pineapple
6-chop loin of pork, chined and skinned	1 cucumber
4 tablespoons cider vinegar	fresh chillies, cut in julienne strips, to garnish

Peel the pineapple from top to bottom in even strips as wide as you can manage and reserve the skin, with the pineapple flesh.

Pound or process together the garlic, peppercorns and coriander roots, adding a little oil if necessary. The larger amount of peppercorns will give rather a hot result, tasting the way Thai food might have done before the arrival of chillies; the smaller amount is probably more acceptable at a family table and, anyway, is rather more fragrant. Rub the mixture into the meat on all sides and tuck some into any cuts and crevices there might be. Cover the fatty top with the strips of pineapple skin. Leave to absorb the flavours for at least an hour at room temperature.

Preheat the oven to 180°C/350°F/Gas 4. Roast the pork for 30 minutes per 450 g (1 lb) plus 30 minutes. Twenty minutes before it is due to be ready, mix together the vinegar, soy and sugar, adjusting the flavour to

your palate. Take the pork from the oven, remove the pineapple skin, and then paint the pork with the sweet and sour sauce. Return to the oven until this has browned nicely and then repeat two or three times more until the pork is cooked through and the outside is lightly caramelized. Let the pork rest for 20 minutes, uncovered.

Meanwhile, make a salad accompaniment by cubing the pineapple flesh and mixing it with half its volume of cucumber (I would peel, halve and seed it and then cut each side thickly into arcs). Add a discreet sprinkling of sliced red or green chilli.

You should have some of the sweet and sour mixture left. Stir that into the baking pan, heat well, scraping the base, strain and serve as a sauce.

STIR-FRIED PORK WITH GARLIC, BLACK PEPPER AND CORIANDER
Khao Mu Tod Krathiam Prik Thai

It would be difficult to imagine any simpler or more essentially Thai dish than this, relying solely on garlic, black pepper and coriander root as its base, and finished with *nam pla* and chillies. The browned garlic, considered unkindly in European cookery, gives a unique, extra sweet-sharp flavour.

SERVES 2–3

350 g (12 oz) lean pork loin	4 black peppercorns
6 small garlic cloves	2 teaspoons nam pla (fish sauce)
2 teaspoons sliced garlic, fried until golden	8 tablespoons vegetable oil
½ teaspoon or more chopped coriander root or plant	TO GARNISH
	sliced fresh red chilli

Slice the pork very thinly. Pound or process together the two garlics, coriander root and peppercorns, adjusting the balance to your preference with more or less of any of the ingredients.

Mix the paste into the pork slices, add the *nam pla* and then mix again. Set aside for 30 minutes at room temperature or for 2 hours in a refrigerator.

Heat the oil over medium heat and then fry the pork until golden brown: remove with a slotted spoon, drain on kitchen towels and serve with thin slices of red chilli and whatever condiments take your fancy.

STEAMED DISHES

One very important thing here. You must cook food to be steamed on a plate or in a container. If you don't, any possible nutritional advantage steaming might have over cooking in liquid is lost: the goodness drips down into the water, dissolved away by the water vapour. Because microwaving is essentially steaming and actually helps save and concentrate both flavour and nutritional value, it is very much the best way of all to cook these dishes.

Even though it is essentially a salad with a dipping sauce, I have included *nam prik* in this chapter because it is a sensational way to serve steamed or microwaved vegetables.

TONGSAI CRAB WITH GARLIC-CHILLI DIP
Pu-Ma Nung Kap Namchim Krathiam Prik Rod-Det

Use whatever boiled or steamed crab you can buy for this: blue crabs would be the Thai choice. At Tongsai Bay on Ko Samui, you can choose to eat them in the bath, as many of the rooms actually have one outside on their terraces, with views and exotic arbours.

SERVES 4–6

2.25 kg (5 lb) cooked crabs

FOR THE DIP
2 teaspoons small hot chillies
2 teaspoons finely chopped garlic

1 teaspoon chopped coriander root or plant
1 teaspoon palm sugar
2 tablespoons fresh lime juice
salt

Pound or process the dip ingredients together until the sugar and salt have dissolved. Let it sit a while, so the flavours develop, and disjoint, chop or cut the crabs into suitable pieces.

Serve with acres of kitchen towels, plus the usual screwdrivers, pliers, hammers and patience needed to extract the crab meat.

GARLIC PRAWNS
Goong Neung Krathiam

This can be cooked and served without much mucking around. One of the many sweet chilli sauces available is the best accompaniment, but the addition of finely sliced chillies or a few shakes of Tabasco does nicely, for those who like the chilli effect but who find themselves without sauces in the pantry.

This recipe can use large or small prawns, raw or cooked and with shells on or off. If they are already shelled the amount of flavouring can be reduced by up to half.

SERVES 4–6

2 tablespoons vegetable oil
½ teaspoon salt
1 teaspoon white pepper
1 teaspoon fresh root ginger, finely chopped
4 large garlic cloves, finely chopped

3 tablespoons chopped fresh coriander plant, including roots
2 tablespoons finely sliced spring onion
450 g (1 lb) prawns

Mix together all the prepared ingredients and then turn the prawns in this. Put them on a plate or in a shallow bowl that will fit in your steamer.

Bring the steamer water to boiling, put the container of prawns over that, cover and steam for 10 minutes if the prawns are raw and in the shell; raw, shelled prawns should take 6–7 minutes. Cooked prawns, which only need heating through, will take just a couple of minutes. Clearly, smaller prawns will take comparatively less time than big ones. These instructions seem complicated, I know, but a few minutes thought and planning avoids rubbery disasters. Microwaving on high for 2–3 minutes (in an 850-watt oven) will steam 450 g (1 lb) of raw prawns with shells on; make the usual adjustments for other types and other sizes.

STIR-FRIED GARLIC PRAWNS
Turn the prawns only in the salt, pepper, ginger and garlic and then stir-fry in vegetable oil until almost done. Then stir in the spring onion and coriander, heating and stirring just until they become vibrantly green.

GRILLED GARLIC PRAWNS

Coated with the mixture of seasonings, ginger and garlic these may be grilled or barbecued and then sprinkled with the herbs. Even better is to use the complete mixture and very large prawns indeed, to wrap them in oiled banana leaf or, if you must, foil, and then to grill or barbecue them like that.

SEA PERCH STEAMED WITH CHILLIES IN LIME SAUCE
Pla Kaphong Khao Neung Prik Sot Manao

A fish of the size suggested is just right for a main course for two people, if you are not eating Thai-style. Sea perch was served at The Thai House but grey mullet or thick fillets of boneless hoki from New Zealand will do very nicely.

At the British Embassy residence in Bangkok, dishes like this are a favourite of HM Ambassador Christian Adams and his wife, when they dine *en famille*. The version they specially like adds even more fragrance, by omitting the stock but adding a tablespoon each of chopped lemon grass and of sliced galangal plus ten or so basil leaves and a couple of tablespoons of Chinese rice wine. It helps to let the fish sit with the ingredients for a while before you steam it.

SERVES 4–6

450 g (1 lb) cleaned weight whole fish	1½ tablespoons light soy sauce
5 hot fresh chillies, chopped	2 spring onions, cut into 2.5 cm
300 ml (10 fl oz) fish, chicken or	(1 inch) lengths
vegetable stock	6 large garlic cloves, peeled but left
3 tablespoons lime juice	whole

Score the flesh of the fish well and put it into an ovenproof dish. Combine the chillies, stock, lime juice and soy sauce and then pour this over the fish. Surround the fish with spring onions and garlic. Put the dish into a prepared steamer, perhaps onto a rack standing in a roasting dish of hot water. You may choose to cover it with a tent of foil or leave the top exposed. Bake for about 20 minutes, or until the fish just flakes nicely. If you have the time, spoon some of the stock over the fish from time to time.

STEAMED FISH CUSTARDS

To demonstrate just how interested Thais are in new culinary ideas, here is a modern, low-calorie version of a very classic style of steamed dish: fundamentally, cubes of fish in a fragrant and spiced custard. At Chiva-Som Health Resort on the Gulf of Siam, they reduce the calorie and cholesterol count by replacing coconut milk and cream with skimmed milk and using only egg whites. Although still commonly cooked in banana leaf cups in the countryside, modern city kitchens opt for ramekins and such. Snapper is an ideal fish, but cod is equally good.

When these steamed custards are more traditionally made in banana leaf cups and with whole eggs and coconut milk, they are called *ho mok*.

Instead of including the Chinese cabbage, you could stir some of the lime leaf and basil into the basic mixture; you might use cubes of chicken or cooked pork instead of fish.

SERVES 6 OR MORE, DEPENDING ON RAMEKIN SIZE

550 g (1¼ lb) white fish fillets, cut in	4 egg whites, lightly beaten
1 cm (½ inch) cubes	225 g (8 oz) Chinese cabbage, finely
2 tablespoons red curry paste	shredded
(pages 15–16)	10 large fresh basil leaves
450 ml (15 fl oz) skimmed milk	3 kaffir lime leaves, finely sliced
3 tablespoons nam pla (fish sauce)	2–3 fresh red chillies, cut in
1 tablespoon palm sugar	julienne strips

Combine the fish and curry paste in a bowl and then gently stir in the milk, *nam pla*, palm sugar and egg whites.

Quickly blanch the Chinese cabbage in boiling water, just until it's wilted and brightened. Drain and cool quickly under cold running water. Drain well and then squeeze to extract as much moisture as possible.

Divide the cabbage between ramekins and sprinkle it with the basil leaves. Spoon in the prepared fish mixture evenly and then top with the lime leaves and chillies.

Steam for about 12 minutes, or until gently set. In an 850-watt microwave, arrange in a circle and cook on medium for 8–10 minutes, checking after 5 minutes. Serve them lukewarm or lightly chilled, and turn them out if you think them firm enough. This is easier if the base of each ramekin is lined with a circle of lightly oiled banana leaf, which should be removed, turned upside-down on the plate and used as a base for each custard.

KAI TUN SONG KRUANG

This is a further variation, made with 4 eggs, 300 ml (10 fl oz) of chicken stock and 6 tablespoons of crab meat, flavoured with a tablespoon each of *nam pla* (fish sauce), coriander leaves and chopped spring onions, plus a little white pepper. Steam or microwave this in individual ramekins and serve warm, topped with extra crab meat, golden fried garlic and a few coriander leaves. Very special.

CHIVA-SOM STEAMED FISH

Simply prepared, this fish is partly steamed, partly poached, because only half of it is in a liquid. The ideal container is a fish-shaped dish just big enough to hold everything, commonly bought in Thailand. As a Western-style main course, this size fish serves three or four, as a first course six or more. Grey mullet is always a good choice for steaming and poaching but sea bass is even better, if it is affordable.

SERVES 4–6

4 dried Chinese mushrooms
750 g (1½ lb) cleaned weight whole fish
1 cm (½ inch) piece of fresh root ginger, shredded
2 spring onions, shredded
1 Chinese celery stalk, or celery leaves and thin stalks, chopped

2 fresh red chillies, cut in julienne *strips*
2 tablespoons finely sliced fresh basil leaves
4 kaffir lime leaves, finely sliced
3 tablespoons nam pla *(fish sauce)*
150 ml (5 fl oz) Chiva-Som Vegetable Stock (page 35)

Preheat the oven to 180°C/350°F/Gas 4. Soak the mushrooms in hot water for 10 minutes and then drain and slice them thinly, discarding the stem. Slash the fish diagonally a couple of times.

Combine the mushrooms, ginger, spring onions, celery, chillies, half the basil and half the lime leaves. Put some of this mixture into the cavity of the fish, and put the fish in a suitable baking dish. Strew the remainder of the mixture over the fish and then mix together the *nam pla* and stock and pour that gently around the fish.

Put the dish into a prepared steamer, perhaps on to a rack standing in a roasting dish of hot water. You may choose to cover it with a tent of foil or leave the top exposed. Bake for about 20 minutes, or until the fish just flakes nicely. If you have the time, spoon some of the stock over the fish from time to time.

Serve garnished with the remaining basil and lime leaves.

LEAF-STEAMED FISH
Pla Yang Bai Toey

The pandanus (fragrant screwpine) leaf adds its particular flavour to the original version, which I ate at Tongsai Bay on Ko Samui. Chef Piengchom Darbanand reckons leek leaves do nicely, too, but so would banana leaf or *in extremis*, foil. Even though this is baked, grilled or barbecued, the wrapping means the fish is, in effect, steamed in its own moisture.

If you can get your fishmonger to bone the fish through the top rather than through the belly, or at least to remove the biggest ones, serving and eating are much more enjoyable. Fresh turmeric, rather a northern Thailand thing, makes a terrific difference to flavour and is worth looking for; otherwise, use half the amount of dried turmeric and a little chopped fresh galangal or ginger.

The best fish to use for this recipe. as before, are sea bass and grey mullet though as usual, you can be inventive here.

SERVES 4–6

450 g (1 lb) cleaned, boned weight whole fish
½ teaspoon salt
2 teaspoons chopped fresh turmeric
4–6 fresh red chillies or to taste

2 teaspoons finely chopped Thai shallot
2 teaspoons finely chopped garlic
pandanus, leek or banana leaves
vegetable oil, if necessary

First rub the fish inside and out with the salt. Pound or process together the turmeric, chillies, shallot and garlic and then stuff this inside the fish. Wrap in your chosen leaves, first lightly oiling them if they are a little inflexible.

Barbecue or grill with medium heat or bake at 180°C/350°F/Gas 4 for 10 minutes per 2.5 cm (1 inch) of thickness, plus 10 minutes; on very hot barbecues, also wrap the fish in foil, which both dramatizes the steamed effect and helps prevent burnt offerings.

Do not attempt to unwrap the fish to serve it; instead, use scissors to cut around the equator of the parcel, thus removing the top and serving it in a fragrant green bed (on a plate or chopping board, of course).

A whole fish, in leaves but no foil, would microwave on high (in an 850-watt oven) in about 5–6 minutes.

NAM PRIK WITH VEGETABLES

Although *nam prik* is, properly, only the chilli/shrimp dipping sauce, the name is also used for the accompanying array of vegetables and fish with which it is eaten. The distinct appeal of *nam prik* is that, when eaten with rice, it provides an almost complete spectrum of protein, vitamins and minerals; add fish and vegetables and there can hardly be a more balanced meal. Thus, as with *Big Salad with Meat and Vegetables* (page 104), you might find yourself serving just this dish, followed by fabulous fruit. *Nam prik* is also admirably suited to being a first course or an appetizer with drinks.

There are no absolute recipes or rules, except that a thick *nam prik* sauce is generally eaten with raw vegetables and a thin one with vegetables either plainly steamed or, rather better, poached in thin coconut milk.

Here are recipes for both, but neither is gospel. If you don't like the flavour of *kapi* or dried shrimps, use much less or none, but don't make the mistake of making a *nam prik* that tastes only of chilli and lime. That's vulgar, and a waste of time and ingredients. If this harsh, unbalanced flavour is what you really like, slice chillies into vinegar and serve that as an accompaniment.

Anything which you would use as a *crudité* is appropriate as an accompaniment but please be creative and keep away from boring carrot and celery. Thais, for instance, would include mint and coriander leaves, spinach and all manner of bean or pea shoots, as well as cucumber, beans, red pepper, baby corn, asparagus spears and such.

THICK NAM PRIK

1 tablespoon kapi *(shrimp paste)*, *roasted*	*palm sugar*
2 tablespoons chopped garlic	*lime juice*
4 tablespoons dried shrimps, pounded	*hot chillies*
175 g (6 oz) cooked, shelled prawns	*1 whole coriander plant, chopped*
nam pla *(fish sauce)*	*(optional)*
	crudités, *to serve*

Make a smooth paste of the *kapi*, garlic, dried shrimps and half of the fresh prawns. Now you must use your initiative, adding the remaining ingredients one by one to achieve the balance which suits you. Expect to use 3 or 4 tablespoons of *nam pla*, slightly more lime juice, about 2 tablespoons of palm sugar and chillies to your taste as a good starting point.

Don't forget that you can temper the chillies by removing the seeds and inner membranes; if they are sliced and only lightly bruised they will be less potent than if they are pounded entirely into the *nam prik*. The inexperienced may find it safer to use Tabasco sauce, sprinkle by sprinkle.

Just before serving, add the remaining prawns, roughly chopped. A whole coriander plant roughly chopped can be added to this for variety.

NAM PRIK WITH FISH
Nam Prik Pla Yaang

This elegant and more complicated version of *nam prik* comes from The Oriental Hotel, where they recommend using the same fish in the paste as you eat with it.

7 small hot red chillies chopped	3 tablespoons lime juice
2 dried red chillies, cut, soaked and drained	2 tablespoons nam pla (fish sauce)
5 garlic cloves, roasted	1 teaspoon palm sugar
5 Thai shallots, roasted	1 teaspoon grated kaffir lime zest
175g (6 oz) flaked, grilled fish	
1 teaspoon kapi (shrimp paste, roasted	TO SERVE
	grilled or fried fish
	raw vegetables

Pound or process together the fresh and dried chillies. Add the garlic and shallots and keep working until you have a fine paste. If you use a processor, it is still worth also pounding the mixture as this definitely makes a better blend of flavours.

Add the flaked fish and *kapi* to the paste, and then mix gently. Gradually stir in the lime juice, *nam pla*, palm sugar and kaffir lime zest.

Serve as above with grilled or fried fish and, to be correct, raw rather than cooked vegetables – carved ones, of course.

THIN NAM PRIK

As it's unlikely you will find the sour-tasting *ma-uk* or *ma-dun* of Thailand, use gooseberries, cooking apple or crab apples for your sour fruit.

1 tablespoon kapi *(shrimp paste),*
roasted
2 tablespoons chopped garlic
1 teaspoon salt
4 tablespoons sour fruit, peeled and
chopped
small hot fresh chillies

nam pla *(fish sauce)*
palm sugar
lime juice

TO SERVE
cooked vegetables
thick coconut cream

Thoroughly combine the *kapi*, garlic and salt and add the sour fruit. Mix these in to make an even paste and then add the chillies, whole but slightly bruised; some would add a couple of dozen, others just a few.

Dilute this with plenty of *nam pla* and then flavour that with palm sugar and lime juice to taste. To keep it thin, you might use twice as much of each as you would for thick *nam prik*. Serve surrounded by boiled, steamed or microwaved vegetables, drizzled with thick coconut cream.

If you fancy cooking the vegetables in coconut milk, go for a mixture of at least four and up to eight. Please don't include carrots or other root vegetables unless your budget insists. Baby corn, beans, pumpkin, sweet potato, spinach leaves and perhaps some sliced bamboo shoots. Start with those that will take longer to cook and add the rest successively.

This thin *nam prik* can also be heated, without the lime juice, and the lightly cooked vegetables added to heat through. Finalize the flavour with freshly squeezed lime juice. This version is much more likely to be served as a single vegetable course with meat, seafood or fish of some sort, making it particularly suited to becoming a distinctive way to go Thai without cooking a big range of dishes.

CURRIES

These are perhaps some of the most popular of all Thai dishes. The recipes for making your own curry pastes or improving bought ones are on pages 14–16. From then on it's really up to you to use the pastes just when and where you like. Please don't forget that the suggested servings are based on these dishes as part of the choice at a typical Thai meal. If you want to serve them as a solo main course, you will need to double the recipe or more.

GREEN CURRY WITH PRAWNS

Kaeng Kheaw Whan Goong

To celebrate its 120th birthday, The Oriental Hotel plans to publish its most popular recipes; this was one of the first that the chefs chose for the book.

SERVES 4–6

8 tablespoons coconut cream
3 tablespoons green curry paste (pages 14–15)
450 ml (15 fl oz) coconut milk
2 kaffir lime leaves, torn
1½ tablespoons nam pla (fish sauce)
1 teaspoon palm sugar

175 g (6 oz) Thai aubergine, cut into 2.5 cm (1 inch) pieces
450 g (1 lb) raw prawns, shelled and de-veined
12 large fresh basil leaves
2 fresh red chillies, cut in julienne strips

Stir the coconut cream in a wok or pan over medium heat until it has an oily sheen. Add the curry paste and then stir continuously for 2 minutes.

Stir in the coconut milk, lime leaves, *nam pla* and sugar and, once the mixture is boiling, stir in the aubergine. Simmer until the aubergine is soft and then add the prawns and cook until they're done, just a few minutes. Stir in the basil and chillies and serve at once.

If you use cooked prawns, stir them in last of all and heat through.

CURRIED PRAWNS
Chu Chi Goong

There will always be the time when you want the combination of Thai flavours and seafood but don't have any curry paste. This is the answer from The Thai Cooking School at The Oriental Hotel, which has taught thousands to cook; as usual, you can add or subtract substantially but still get a good-tasting dish.

SERVES 4–6

9 large dried chillies
7 garlic cloves, chopped
5 Thai shallots, chopped
1 tablespoon finely sliced lemon grass
3 slices of fresh galangal
1 teaspoon kapi (shrimp paste)
½ teaspoon salt
vegetable oil, for frying
450 g (1 lb) raw prawns, shelled and de-veined

300 ml (10 fl oz) coconut milk
150 ml (5 fl oz) coconut cream
1 teaspoon palm sugar
2 tablespoons nam pla (fish sauce)

TO GARNISH
fresh chillies, cut in julienne strips
kaffir lime leaves, cut in julienne strips

Soak the chillies in warm water for about 5 minutes or until softened; then drain them. Chop the chillies and then pound or process them, together with the garlic, shallots, lemon grass and galangal, until well combined. Then mix in the kapi and salt.

Quickly stir-fry the prawns in hot oil until they no longer look raw and then drain them on absorbent paper.

Bring the mixed coconut milk and cream to the boil and then stir in the prepared paste. Simmer gently until it is reduced to a rich, coating consistency. Stir the sugar and nam pla into the mixture and then add the prawns, heating them just until they are cooked through.

Serve at once, strewn with shredded chillies and lime leaves.

ROAST DUCK RED CURRY
Kaeng Phed Ped Yaang

Provided you live close to a Chinese take-away to provide the red-cooked duck, this best-of-all Thai curries is a cinch to make. The hardest part is deciding whether to include cherry tomatoes, pineapple, lychees, pea-aubergines . . . or what. There should, ideally, be something sharp and savoury and something sweet. This recipe is an amalgam of many I have tasted and made. The secret is not to heat it too long before serving or the duck might lose its flavour to the liquid and taste like cardboard.

You can finish this in a variety of ways. As a guide, The Oriental Hotel uses tomato wedges and finishes the curry with white grapes or lychees; a royal Thai version I enjoyed included cherry tomatoes, aubergines and pineapple; at the Sukhothai Hotel, it contained pea aubergines and apple slices.

SERVES 4–6

1 Chinese red-roasted duck
12 tablespoons coconut cream
3 tablespoons red curry paste
(pages 15–16)
450 ml (15 fl oz) coconut milk
3 large tomatoes, cut in wedges, or
10 cherry tomatoes, or 175 g (6 oz)
pea aubergines, green peas or sliced
green beans
12 green grapes or 12 cubes of fresh
pineapple or a thickly sliced
sharp apple

4 kaffir lime leaves, torn or finely
sliced
2 tablespoons nam pla (fish sauce)
½ teaspoon salt
1 teaspoon palm sugar

TO GARNISH
fresh basil leaves
fresh red chillies, cut in julienne
strips

First, take all the flesh from the cooked duck and cut it into elegant strips, or into cubes of about 5 cm (2 inches), keeping the skin on as many pieces as possible.

Stir 8 tablespoons of the coconut cream over medium heat until hot; then mix in the curry paste and continue stirring for 2 minutes. Add the duck, coconut milk, your choice of vegetables and fruit, the lime leaves, nam pla, salt and sugar and then bring slowly to the boil, by which time everything will be heated through. Serve swirled with the remaining thick coconut cream and sprinkled with basil leaves and julienne of red chillies.

PORK RED CURRY WITH GREEN BEANS
Phat Prik Khing Mu Kap Thua Fak Yao

Provided you keep the beans green and crisp, this looks brilliantly colourful. When I watched this made at The Thai House, the beans were barely blanched, yet by the time the dish was finally assembled and served, they were just right. Yard-long or snake beans are correct but other kinds do nicely.

SERVES 4–6

225 g (8 oz) green beans, cut in
2.5 cm (1 inch) lengths
2 tablespoons red curry paste
(pages 15–16)
2 tablespoons dried shrimps, ground
3 tablespoons vegetable oil

450 g (1 lb) lean pork loin, thinly
sliced
1 tablespoon palm sugar
1 tablespoon nam pla (fish sauce)
3 kaffir lime leaves, finely sliced

Blanch the prepared beans in boiling water for just long enough to brighten the colour. Quickly cool them in cold running water, drain well and reserve. Combine the red curry paste and dried shrimps.

Heat the oil in a large wok or pan over medium heat and then stir-fry the pork until it's cooked through. Remove and cover.

Stir-fry the curry paste mixture in the same oil for 2 minutes or until fragrant. Add the cooked pork, sugar, nam pla and beans and then stir-fry until they're evenly mixed and heated through. Stir through the lime leaves and serve.

GREEN CHICKEN CURRY
Kaeng Kheaw Whan Kai Chiva-som

Perhaps one of Thailand's most popular dishes and thus one which everyone makes in their own way. This version is very special, though, made for those who think they should avoid or reduce the calories in coconut milk and cream. Chiva-Som Health Resort makes it with skimmed milk and stock, and remarkably tasty it is too.

SERVES 3–4

8 tablespoons Chiva-Som Vegetable Stock (page 35)
3 teaspoons green curry paste (pages 14–15)
400 g (14 oz) boneless, skinless chicken breast, cubed or sliced
5 fresh green chillies, cut in julienne strips
15 large fresh basil leaves

100 g (4 oz) pea aubergines
100 g (4 oz) white aubergine, cubed
1 tablespoon nam pla (fish sauce)
250 ml (8 fl oz) skimmed milk
4 kaffir lime leaves, torn

TO GARNISH
fresh chillies, cut in julienne strips
fresh basil leaves

Add 2 tablespoons of the stock to a wok or pan; stir in the curry paste and then cook over medium heat until the mixture is almost dry. Turn the chicken into the paste and then add the chillies, basil, aubergines and nam pla.

Simmer the mixture for about 7 minutes and then stir in the milk and cook on until the chicken is cooked through and tender. Mix through the lime leaves and serve garnished with extra shredded chillies and basil leaves.

VARIATION: For the more usual style, make the curry in exactly the same way, but add as much or up to twice as much coconut cream or coconut milk, rather than skimmed milk. In either version, the aubergines can be replaced with whatever takes your fancy, or left out altogether.

CHICKEN CURRY WITH BAMBOO AND CUCUMBER
Kaeng Phet Kat Sai No Mai

This is another of the curries we savoured at The Thai House. Choose red or green curry paste according to what else is being served at the meal, so you have a good spectrum of flavours. I added the cucumber, which is often seen cooked in Thai dishes, because its texture neatly bridges that of the bamboo shoots and the meat, as well as adding a little colour.

This curry lends itself to becoming a very gently spiced dish; if that is your wish, use only a tablespoon of curry paste and omit the fresh chillies.

Large shelled prawns will happily substitute for the chicken: put them in last, so they do not overcook. And, because this is Thai cooking, you can leave out the bamboo shoots and the cucumber, too, and just make a rich, mild prawn curry. Or chicken curry. Or fish.

SERVES 4–6

250 ml (8 fl oz) coconut cream
2 tablespoons green or red curry paste
(pages 14–16)
750 g (1½ lb) boneless, skinless
chicken breast
225 g (8 oz) cucumber
100 g (4 oz) canned bamboo shoots,
thinly sliced
3 tablespoons nam pla (fish sauce)

1 tablespoon palm sugar
8 kaffir lime leaves, halved
1–2 fresh red chillies, cut in julienne
strips
30 fresh basil leaves

TO GARNISH
fresh basil leaves
thinly sliced lemon grass (optional)

Bring the coconut cream to the boil in a wok or frying-pan and then continue cooking until oil rises to the surface. Add the curry paste and cook until fragrant; reduce the heat and simmer. Slice the chicken breasts lengthways, getting 4–5 pieces per breast. Add the pieces to the hot mixture and continue simmering until tender, about 15 minutes.

Meanwhile, halve the cucumber lengthways and remove the seeds. Cut each half into arc-shaped slices, as thick or thin as you wish but making a contrast to the bamboo shoot slices.

A few minutes before serving, add the cucumber and remaining ingredients, heating through until the cucumber becomes slightly transparent but still crunchy. Garnish with basil and very thinly sliced lemon grass.

YELLOW CURRIED CHICKEN THIGHS
Kaeng Kari Kai

This recipe from The Thai House clearly sits on the border between Thai and Indian curries. Go for a bigger flavour, but less attractive look, by using whole thighs or other chicken pieces, with the bone in, and cook them for a little longer.

SERVES 4–6

500 ml (17 fl oz) coconut cream
2 tablespoons red curry paste
(pages 15–16)
1 tablespoon curry powder
100 g (4 oz) onion, finely chopped
450 g (1 lb) skinless, boneless chicken thighs, cut in 5 cm (2 inch) pieces
750 ml (1¼ pints) coconut milk

225 g (8 oz) potato, cut in 2.5 cm (1 inch) cubes
3 tablespoons nam pla *(fish sauce)*
1 tablespoon palm sugar

TO GARNISH
fresh coriander leaves (optional)

Bring half the coconut cream slowly to the boil in a wok or pan over medium heat. Add the combined curry paste and powder, return to a gentle boil, and then gradually add the remaining coconut cream, stirring constantly, until oil rises to surface.

Mix in the onion and cook until it's well softened; add the chicken and stir for a few minutes, until it no longer looks raw.

Stir in the coconut milk, potato, *nam pla* and sugar. Bring to the boil and then reduce the heat to a simmer and cook, covered, until the chicken is tender and the potato cooked (20–30 minutes).

You might like to scatter on some coriander leaves as garnish when serving.

GREEN BEEF CURRY
Kaeng Khiao Wan Neua

Purists often say beef should not be cooked with a green paste, reckoning it might taste good but doesn't look well. Perhaps so, but it is increasingly found and very popular. Best to judge for yourself.

SERVES 4–6

2 tablespoons vegetable oil
2–3 tablespoons green curry paste
(pages 14–15)
750 g (1½ lb) lean chuck steak or
similar, cubed or sliced
1 litre (1¾ pints) coconut milk
4 kaffir lime leaves, torn
1½ teaspoons palm sugar

2 tablespoons nam pla (fish sauce)
25 large fresh basil leaves, cut in
julienne strips
2 fresh red chillies, cut in julienne
strips

TO GARNISH
fresh coriander leaves

Heat the oil in a wok and fry the green curry paste over gentle heat until it's fragrant. Add the beef, turn up the heat a little and stir-fry until the beef no longer looks raw. Pour on the coconut milk. Bring it to the boil and then reduce the heat to a simmer. Add the lime leaves, palm sugar and *nam pla* and continue simmering, uncovered, until the beef is tender, which could be 45 minutes or more.

Stir in the basil leaves, with the chillies, just before serving. Garnish with coriander leaves.

VARIATIONS: Some cooks make this much richer by starting with 2 litres (3½ pints) of coconut milk, which they reduce by half before doing anything else. If you use the above recipe but want something richer, stir in extra coconut cream.

If you like the flavour of pea aubergines, add about 100 g (4 oz) once the coconut milk has come to the boil; cubes of other Thai aubergines (not of the large Mediterranean type) can be substituted.

VEGETARIAN JUNGLE CURRY
Kaeng Paa

This is supposedly so named because it is the sort of food a traveller might make with what he found in the jungle, plus such staples as *kapi* that could be carried. Its particular advantage is that it does not include coconut – there are few in the jungle – and that the basic method can be used to cook anything: fish, fowl, beast or vegetable. In these more diet-conscious days, I thought you would appreciate a vegetable version.

In the absence of lemon grass, more kaffir lime leaves or its peel might be used. As usual in Thai cookery, it's up to you, whether your jungle is tropical or suburban. If you were really in the jungle, wild turmeric or krachai would be popped into the pot, too.

SERVES 4–6

2 tablespoons chopped lemon grass
1 tablespoon chopped Thai shallot
½ tablespoon chopped garlic
1 coriander plant, including roots, chopped
1 tablespoon chopped fresh galangal
1 teaspoon kaffir lime zest
2–4 dried red chillies
1 teaspoon salt
2 tablespoons vegetable oil
1 litre (1¾ pints) stock or water
175 g (6 oz) green beans, cut in 5 cm (2 inch) lengths
225 g (8 oz) pumpkin, cut in 2.5 cm (1 inch) cubes

175 g (6 oz) baby corn cobs, cut in 5 cm (2 inch) lengths
6 dried Chinese mushrooms, soaked
225 g (8 oz) firm bean curd, cut in 2.5 cm (1 inch) cubes, or 4 hard-boiled eggs, shelled and quartered lengthways
2 kaffir lime leaves, torn

TO SERVE
light soy sauce
fresh coriander leaves, roughly torn
fresh basil leaves, roughly torn
fresh chillies, cut in julienne strips

Combine the first eight ingredients, using a mortar and pestle or food processor. Stir-fry the resultant paste in the oil for a minute over medium heat, and then add the stock or water, beans, pumpkin and corn. Drain the mushrooms, discarding the stalks, and then cut into quarters.

When the vegetables are tender, add the mushrooms and the bean curd or eggs, plus the lime leaves. Gently heat through and serve with light soy sauce and bowls of torn coriander, basil leaves and shredded fresh chillies.

PENANG BEEF IN SWEET PEANUT SAUCE
Pha-Naeng Neua

The influence of Thailand's neighbour Malaysia is clear in both the name of this recipe and the inclusion of peanuts. If you should find something called Panang or Pha-naeng curry paste, it is essentially red curry paste with peanuts or peanut butter in it; use that instead, and reduce the peanuts that you add a little. But this is the version I ate at The Thai House, only 45 minutes by canal boat from central Bangkok but genuinely rural. You can stay there while you learn to cook family dishes every day.

SERVES 4–6

750 ml (1¼ pints) coconut milk
750 g (1½ lb) chuck or rump steak, cut in thin strips
600 ml (1 pint) coconut cream
3 tablespoons red curry paste (page 15–16)
6 kaffir lime leaves, finely shredded
75–100 g (3–4 oz) dry-roasted peanuts, ground

2 tablespoons nam pla (fish sauce)
1 tablespoon palm sugar
2 fresh red chillies, cut in julienne strips
15 large fresh basil leaves, plus a few extra to garnish (optional)

Bring 600 ml (1 pint) of the coconut milk to the boil in a wok or pan, and then stir in the beef. Simmer, uncovered, until the beef is tender and the coconut milk is very thick. Chuck steak will take about 45 minutes; remove rump steak after 10–15 minutes and continue simmering the coconut milk until it is really thick, being careful not to burn it.

Pour a third of the coconut cream into another wok or pan. Boil until the oil has risen to the surface. Reserve 2 tablespoons of the cream. Stir the curry paste into the cream in the wok and then slowly add the remaining two-thirds of the coconut cream, stirring continuously, until the mixture has an oily sheen. Stir in the prepared beef with the reduced coconut milk, the lime leaves and remaining thin coconut milk. Stir over the heat until everything is well combined.

Add the peanuts, nam pla, sugar and chillies. Finely slice the basil leaves and stir them through. When thoroughly heated through, serve garnished with swirls of the reserved 2 tablespoons of thick coconut cream. A few extra basil leaves would look nice, too.

MUSLIM BEEF CURRY
Kaeng Mussaman

This is the only Thai curry which uses such sweet spices as cinnamon, cloves and cardamom, indicative of Indian or Sri Lankan influence on the western coast, whence it comes.

The onions can be replaced with fresh pineapple chunks or 3–4 tablespoons of dry-roasted peanuts; a scatter of chopped peanuts makes an interesting garnish to the basic recipe.

You can also prepare chicken and duck joints with these flavourings, perhaps without the potato; this makes a quantity more suited to a Thai-style meal of several dishes than to a single main course.

SERVES 6–8

4 tablespoons vegetable oil
1 kg (2¼ lb) chuck or other stewing beef, cut in 5 cm (2 inch) cubes
1 tablespoon nam pla (fish sauce)
1 litre (1¾ pints) coconut milk
450 g (1 lb) small whole onions or Thai shallots
450 g (1 lb) potatoes, cut in 5 cm (2 inch) cubes

3 tablespoons red curry paste (pages 15–16)
6 cloves
4 cardamom pods, lightly crushed
1 cinnamon stick
1 teaspoon aniseed or fennel seeds
6–8 tablespoons tamarind water (pages 22–23)
2–3 tablespoons palm sugar

Heat half the oil in a wok or pan and fry the beef cubes until they're well browned. Stir in a teaspoon of the *nam pla* and half the coconut milk. Simmer, covered, until the beef is tender, about 45 minutes.

Heat the remaining oil in a wok or pan and then lightly brown the onions or shallots and potatoes, which helps stop them from disintegrating. Remove the browned vegetables and reserve the oil.

Gently fry the combined curry paste and spices in the reserved oil, until they're very lightly browned. Add the remaining coconut milk, the beef and its cooking liquid, plus the browned vegetables, and stir in some of the tamarind water and sugar. Leave to simmer for 20 minutes, or until the vegetables are tender, stirring only if absolutely necessary. Adjust the flavour with the remaining *nam pla*, tamarind water and sugar, to perfect a satisfying blend of sweet and savoury.

RICE AND NOODLES

Everything in this chapter is a one-dish meal, more often enjoyed during the day rather than at night, unless all you want is a light supper. At authentic Thai meals with a choice of cooked dishes, only plain rice is usually served and noodles are more likely to appear as part of a salad. Basic rice and noodle preparation guides are on pages 21–2.

FRIED RICE
Khao Pad

Fried rice is enjoyed by Thais as a one-dish meal or snack. The best rice for this is at least one day old and has been allowed to dry a little. The way to do this is to spread cooked rice over the base of a tray or large baking dish and then refrigerate it overnight. Allow about 100 g (4 oz) per person cooked weight; 225 g (8 oz) dry weight will make enough cooked rice for four to six people. Here are some of your options, all using that amount of rice.

RED CURRY RICE

Fry 1 or more tablespoons of red curry paste (pages 15–16) in oil until fragrant and then add up to 225 g (8 oz) of sliced cooked meat or 350 g (12 oz) of sliced uncooked chicken or shelled prawns. When they are cooked or heated through, add the rice and stir and turn until evenly coated. Flavour lightly with *nam pla* (fish sauce) or salt. Add a few green vegetables – green beans always work well – and then serve. A favourite combination is pork with fried rice and this is sometimes given a special Thai twist by the last-minute addition of basil leaves: anything up to 40 large ones.

SEAFOOD FRIED RICE

Fry a couple of sliced garlic cloves in oil, together with two or more beaten eggs. Once the egg is set, add the rice and stir to mix well. Then flavour with *nam pla* or salt and a few finely sliced chillies or some Tabasco sauce. Now gently mix in up to 350 g (12 oz) of cooked seafood: crab meat, prawns, mussels, etc. When heated through, serve sprinkled with very finely sliced lemon grass bulb or lime leaf, plus some lemon or lime wedges, tomato and cucumber.

PINEAPPLE FRIED RICE

A party dish that pops up all through Asia. First, cut a third from the side of a pineapple in one piece, top to bottom. Scoop the flesh out of this and out of the main body of the pineapple; discard the woody central stem and then cube the remainder. Reserve. Fry the cooked rice in oil, with a few chopped garlic cloves and a couple of teaspoons of green curry paste (pages 14–15), until the grains are heated through and glistening. Then add about 175 g (6 oz) of the chopped fresh pineapple flesh and about the same amount of cooked ham, chicken, turkey or duck. Flavour with *nam pla* (fish sauce) or salt and stir in a few chillies or sprinkle with Tabasco sauce, if the curry paste is not hot enough for you. You can serve this as it is but it is usually stuffed back into the pineapple and kept hot in the oven before serving, or zapped in a microwave. Finish by sprinkling it with a couple of tablespoons of chopped toasted nuts and at least that much sliced garlic, fried until lightly golden brown – and coriander leaves, of course.

NAM PRIK RICE

Follow the recipe for Kapi *Rice* (page 84), using a prepared *Thick* Nam Prik *Sauce* (pages 65–6) instead of *kapi* (shrimp paste), or merely fry rice and flavour it with *Thick* or *Thin* Nam Prik *Sauce*.

KAPI RICE
Khao Kluk Kapi

You either love or hate the flavour of *kapi*, Thai shrimp paste. There seems no middle ground. But this, at least, is a level playing field upon which to make up your mind. Essentially, it is boiled rice flavoured with the paste and typical Thai herbs, to serve as a quick meal for a few or a snack for more. It's pretty good without the *kapi*, too.

SERVES 4–6

450 g (1 lb) Thai fragrant (jasmine) rice
2 eggs, beaten
150 ml (5 fl oz) vegetable oil
8 tablespoons chopped garlic
2 tablespoons kapi (shrimp paste)
1–2 tablespoons cayenne pepper, or Tabasco sauce to taste
6 Thai shallots, sliced
4 tablespoons thinly sliced lemon grass

4 tablespoons nam pla (fish sauce)
4 tablespoons lime juice
4 tablespoons white or palm sugar

TO GARNISH

4 fresh red chillies, cut in julienne strips
8 tablespoons chopped fresh coriander
2 tablespoons fresh mint

Cook the rice and then keep it hot. Meanwhile, cook a thin layer of egg in a non-stick pan until well set. Allow the omelette to cool slightly, roll it up and then slice it thinly and reserve.

Cook the garlic in the hot oil until golden brown, and then stir in the *kapi*, cook for a minute and remove from the heat.

Mix the garlic and *kapi* into the cooked rice and add the cayenne pepper or Tabasco sauce, shallots, lemon grass, *nam pla*, lime juice and sugar. Spoon the mixture into a suitable, lightly oiled mould, press lightly and then turn out on to a serving plate. You can also mould this in individual cups.

Garnish with the sliced omelette, chillies, coriander and mint leaves.

CHICKEN-TOPPED RICE
Khao Na Kai

One of the all-time-favourite one-dish meals, at any time of day. Arguments rage over which stall on which Bangkok street serves this best; every time you make it you'll find you change this or that ingredient until you, too, develop a recipe of your own.

SERVES 1–2

75 g (3 oz) Thai fragrant (jasmine) rice
1½ teaspoons dark soy sauce
2 teaspoons light soy sauce
1 teaspoon sesame oil
1 tablespoon cornflour
1–2 tablespoons Chinese oyster sauce
225 g (8 oz) boneless, skinless chicken breast, cubed
4 tablespoons vegetable oil
about 150 ml (5 fl oz) chicken stock

½ teaspoon white or palm sugar
¼ teaspoon salt
ground white pepper

TO SERVE
fresh red chillies, cut in julienne strips
sliced cucumber
fresh coriander leaves

Cook the rice and keep it hot: if you have leftover rice, the equivalent is 2–3 big cups full of cooked rice.

Mix together the soy sauces, sesame oil, cornflour and a tablespoon of the oyster sauce. Marinate the chicken in this mixture, mixing well, for at least an hour.

Stir-fry the chicken in the hot oil until browned and cooked through. Stir in enough stock to make a thickish sauce, bring back to the boil and then season to your personal taste, using the remaining oyster sauce, the sugar, salt, pepper and perhaps some extra stock. There should be a predominant taste of soy and oyster sauces. Serve over the hot jasmine rice, garnished with your choice of sliced chillies, cucumber and coriander leaves.

DRUNKEN MACARONI
Macaroni Khi Mao

Pasta is suddenly fashionable amongst the bright, young, mobile-telephone brigade of Bangkok, who have taken to this new dish to refresh and revitalize their palates when they are drunk. As you are far more likely to have pasta than rice noodles in your cupboard, it's a great choice for entertaining, even if only yourself.

A contrasting selection of young vegetables may also be added to the mixture, before or after the prawns, according to their size, thus making a substantial dish which can be a meal in itself.

SERVES 2–4

75 g (3 oz) dry weight macaroni
5 tablespoons vegetable oil
about 6 fresh chillies
4 Thai shallots, roughly chopped
2 tablespoons chopped garlic
½ teaspoon kapi (shrimp paste)

450 g (1 lb) raw prawns, shelled and de-veined
1 teaspoon white or palm sugar
2 tablespoons nam pla (fish sauce)
4 tablespoons fresh basil leaves

Cook the macaroni in a pan of boiling, salted water until tender. Drain and then let it rest for a minute or so before turning in a tablespoon of the oil, to moisten. Cover to keep warm.

Pound or process together the chillies, shallots, garlic and *kapi*. Fry this chilli paste in the remaining hot oil until fragrant. Add the prawns and stir-fry them until cooked through. Add the sugar, *nam pla*, macaroni and basil leaves. Adjust the seasoning with *nam pla* and sugar until it is spicy and salty but not sweet. If you use cooked prawns, add them last and just let them heat through.

RICE AND SEAFOOD IN BROTH
Khao Tom

I know, this is more of a soup, but, because it is commonly enjoyed through-out Thailand as a meal in itself rather than as part of a bigger dinner, I felt it more properly belonged to this chapter. The stock you make first is an excellent base for all sorts of other dishes, Thai or Western. But, first and foremost, this stew of fish and rice is one of the most gratifying suppers I know. The amount of fish can be greatly increased to make this look like a chunky stew rather than lumpy soup once it is served.

SERVES 6–8

2 large heads of garlic
2 large whole coriander plants, including roots, or equivalent
1 tablespoon black peppercorns
4 Chinese celery stalks or celery leaves and thin stalks
1 tablespoon cider vinegar
1 tablespoon salt
2.25 litres (4 pints) cold water
1 kg (2¼ lb) mixed fish and seafood

vegetable oil, for frying
225 g (8 oz) Thai fragrant (jasmine) rice
nam pla (fish sauce)

TO SERVE
lime juice
fresh chillies, cut in julienne strips
Chinese celery, coriander or basil leaves

Smash the cloves of one of the heads of garlic and put them into a large saucepan with the coriander, peppercorns, celery, vinegar and salt. Add the water and bring it very slowly to the boil. Meanwhile, peel and slice finely the cloves of the other garlic head and reserve them.

Ideally, the fish in your mixture should be complete with bones and/or heads but no gills. Cook the fish gently in the stock, remove it and, once you have flaked the flesh away in big pieces, reserve the head and bones. Cook anything with shells next and also remove them from the stock. Take the flesh from these, too. Put the bones, heads, shells, etc. back into the stock and simmer for no more than 20 minutes. Strain the stock and put it back into the same saucepan, ideally after washing it.

In a small frying-pan, fry the remaining garlic in the oil until golden brown, then turn the rice in this mixture, without letting the garlic burn. Tip the rice into the stock and cook for 20 minutes or so until the rice is tender. Taste and correct the seasoning with nam pla or salt.

Serve this by putting a selection of the reserved fish and seafood into individual bowls and then ladling the hot rice and stock mixture on to that. Each guest adjusts the flavour to their inner satisfaction by adding more or less of the accompaniments.

RICE NOODLES WITH SPICED PORK SAUCE
Khanom Jean Nam Ngeow

Mom Luang Chiratorn's 200-year-old family compound in Bangkok still sports elephant steps – used to mount these royal beasts of burden for journeys to and from the palace compound. Taught to cook by his grandmother, M.L. Chiratorn has been a restaurateur in Bangkok but now cooks only for pleasure, especially delighting in such noodle dishes as this.

You could, of course, use other types of noodle, if they are easier to obtain.

SERVES 4–6

1 tablespoon chopped coriander root
or plant
2 tablespoons chopped garlic
1½ teaspoons black peppercorns,
roughly crushed
½ tablespoon chopped Thai shallot
9 dried red chillies, soaked and seeded
1 tablespoon kapi (shrimp paste)
4 tablespoons vegetable oil
450 g (1 lb) minced pork

450 g (1 lb) belly of pork (spare ribs), cut in 2.5 cm (1 inch) pieces
nam pla (fish sauce)
450 g (1 lb) firm but very ripe tomatoes, chopped
450 g (1 lb) rice-flour vermicelli

TO GARNISH
fresh coriander leaves
chopped spring onions

Pound together or process the coriander, garlic, peppercorns, shallot, chillies and kapi and then fry this mixture in the hot oil until fragrant.

Add the mince and the belly of pork and keep cooking until they are well browned and cooked through. Mix in nam pla to taste and the tomatoes. Add just enough water to cover and then put the lid on your wok or saucepan. Bring to the boil and simmer for 30–40 minutes until the belly of pork is tender. Adjust the seasoning with nam pla.

When ready to serve, pour boiling water over the vermicelli, drain, then arrange on a serving plate and spoon the mixture over. Garnish with coriander and spring onions.

RICE NOODLES WITH FISH AND VEGETABLES

Khanom Chine Namya Paktai

A beautiful-looking and nutritionally ideal balance: the perfect one-dish meal. You could use three or so tablespoons of a fragrant green curry paste, rather than starting from scratch. But this recipe is the way of Chef Chom of Tongsai Bay, who was formerly a private cook to a senior member of the Thai Royal Family. The rhythmic pounding of fresh ingredients into pastes every-day is one of the many threads that still binds together every facet of Thai society, high or low, in town or country. This might be served as a light meal for up to four or as a first course for more.

Be brave in choosing your selection of vegetables for the stir-fry. Mix mass-es of basil leaves into a stir-fry that for once does not include onion and car-rot! And include something raw or only lightly cooked, cucumber sticks for instance, or pea shoots.

SERVES 2–4

2 tablespoons sliced Thai shallots
1 tablespoon sliced garlic
1 teaspoon sliced fresh galangal
2 tablespoons sliced lemon grass
up to 4 tablespoons dried red chillies,
soaked
1 teaspoon sliced fresh turmeric
1 teaspoon sliced coriander root or
plant
1 teaspoon salt
300 ml (10 fl oz) coconut milk

300 ml (10 fl oz) coconut cream
225 g (8 oz) cooked fish, flaked
2 tablespoons nam pla (fish sauce)
4 kaffir lime leaves, torn

TO SERVE

450 g (1 lb) Thai rice noodles,
cooked
450 g (1 lb) mixed vegetables,
stir-fried

Pound or process together the shallots, garlic, galangal, lemon grass, chillies, turmeric, coriander and salt. Don't forget that it is fine to rinse away the fiery seeds of the chillies, once they have reconstituted.

Fry the paste over medium heat until it's nicely fragrant and then slow-ly stir in the coconut milk and cream. Heat gently until it comes to the boil. Remove from the heat and add the fish, *nam pla* and lime leaves.

Put the prepared noodles into a large bowl (they do not need to have been kept hot) and then pour on the sauce. Garnish with the vegetables.

THE ORIENTAL HOTEL'S STIR-FRIED NOODLES

Guay Tiaw Pad Oriental

Frankly, you can probably cook this sort of dish with your eyes closed; not because it doesn't require skill, but because almost anything can go into it: it's the ultimate catch-all dish, great as a light meal. This is what you will learn if you go to the appropriate class at The Thai Cooking School at The Oriental; it's actually simpler to achieve than many such dishes from less august sources.

SERVES 2–3

2 eggs, lightly beaten
2 tablespoons chopped fresh red chillies
2 tablespoons chopped Thai shallots
3 tablespoons vegetable oil
2 tablespoons nam pla (fish sauce)
1 tablespoon palm sugar
3 tablespoons tamarind water (pages 22–3)
1 teaspoon lime juice
225 g (8 oz) small, raw or cooked, shelled prawns
225 g (8 oz) rice noodles, cooked

TO GARNISH

2 tablespoons dry-roasted peanuts, roughly chopped
2 tablespoons firm bean curd, cubed and fried
2 tablespoons dried shrimps, fried
bean sprouts or pea shoots

First make a thin omelette of the egg and reserve it; ensure you have prepared all the other ingredients that need to be made ready.

Pound or process together the chillies and shallots and then fry them in the oil, together with the *nam pla*, sugar, tamarind water and lime juice (use a little extra lime juice if you can't get tamarind water). After a minute it should all seem wonderfully fragrant, at which stage, add first the prawns and let them cook through, if necessary, and then the prepared noodles. Toss together well, perhaps using two forks. Dump all this on to one end of the prepared omelette, roll it up and then serve garnished with the peanuts, bean curd, dried shrimps and as many bean sprouts or pea shoots as you can face.

VARIATION: You can add finely sliced chillies and whole coriander leaves to the mixture itself before serving.

Home cooks in the city and country folk are more likely to make a more robust version, using only one wok to do everything. Using the same ingredients as above, fry the sliced shallots with as much sliced garlic as you fancy until golden brown and then add prawns, pork or a mixture and flavour with cayenne pepper or with Tabasco sauce and the other flavourings. Once everything is ready, push the contents of the wok to one side – a very large pan would do as well – add more oil and then stir the noodles in the hot oil until well heated through. Push them also to the side and in the base of the wok, cook two or more eggs in a thin layer and, when set, stir everything together. Serve topped with the same peanuts, bean curd and dried shrimps, perhaps also adding coriander and spring onion. If you are familiar with such oddities as banana blossom or Chinese leek, this is the place to serve them.

SALADS

These are nothing whatsoever to do with salads as we know them. Thai salads never have oil on them but are always dressed with something piquant and challenging. They can be made out of anything from raw beef to cooked fish, from fruit and vegetables to roots, shoots and leaves – and virtually any combination of any of them. The Thais are said to eat over 200 raw ingredients alone in their salads, many of them still found growing wild. Once you have the taste for Thai salads, be bold. These recipes are also worth exploring as fascinating first courses or light meals.

PRAWN AND POMELO SALAD
Yam Goong So-O

Andrew Jacka, Executive Chef at Chiva-Som, makes a number of variations on this salad, sometimes using much more honey and then balancing the sweetness with lemon or lime juice. You could, of course, also use fresh chillies rather than dried.

SERVES 2–4

300 g (11 oz) pomelo or grapefruit segments
200 g (7 oz) cooked small prawns, shelled and de-veined
1 teaspoon honey
2 teaspoons nam pla *(fish sauce)*
1 garlic clove, crushed

1 tablespoon finely chopped Thai shallot
5 cm (2 inch) piece of lemon grass bulb, finely sliced
3 dried chillies, sliced
2 tablespoons chopped fresh coriander

Combine the pomelo, prawns, honey, *nam pla* and garlic in a bowl. Stir in the remaining ingredients. Cover and then leave to stand for an hour before serving, to allow the flavours to develop.

POMELO SALAD WITH PORK
Yam So-O

A challenging mixture of seafood, meat and fruit that looks and tastes quite wonderful. But it's not as foreign as you might think; fish and meat or meat and fruit are basic to much Arabic, Moorish and thus Spanish cooking and were commonplace in medieval European cookery. So these combinations might be thought of as rediscoveries rather than discoveries.

SERVES 4–6

175 g (6 oz) cooked prawns, shelled and de-veined
2 tablespoons fresh lime juice
2 tablespoons nam pla *(fish sauce)*
2 tablespoons chilli jam (page 12)
2 tablespoons palm sugar
4 tablespoons chopped roasted pork
2 tablespoons desiccated coconut, roasted

about 150 ml (5 fl oz) coconut cream
1 pomelo or grapefruit, flesh only, shredded

TO GARNISH
shredded fresh basil leaves
chopped fresh red chilli
chopped fresh coriander leaves

Mince half of the prawns. Combine the lime juice, *nam pla*, chilli jam and sugar in a bowl. Stir in the minced prawns, pork, coconut and coconut cream; mix well. Stir in the pomelo or grapefruit and then toss lightly until everything is nicely coated; you might need to add a little extra coconut cream.

Serve topped with the remaining prawns and garnished with basil, chillies and coriander. You could present this in the shells of the pomelo or grapefruit, which is the way they would do it at The Oriental.

THAI BROCCOLI SALAD

Created at Chiva-Som Health Resort from ingredients grown in Thongchai Kunchaiwong's gardens, this salad is meant to be rigorously crisp and raw; if this is asking too much, either briefly blanch whatever type of broccoli you use or let the salad stand for an least an hour, which also eases the effect.

Chinese *choy sum*, or flowering cabbage, is a good substitute for Thai broccoli; ordinary broccoli, cut into small pieces and then elegantly sliced or cut into large matchsticks, is just as nice.

SERVES 4–6

up to 4 small hot fresh chillies, finely chopped
2 garlic cloves, crushed
2 teaspoons nam pla *(fish sauce)*
4 tablespoons fresh lime juice
½ teaspoon palm sugar

225 g (8 oz) Thai broccoli
50 g (2 oz) carrot, cut in, cut in julienne strips
50 g (2 oz) tomato, cut in julienne *strips*

Combine the chillies, garlic, *nam pla*, lime juice and sugar in a bowl; then stir until the sugar is dissolved. Stir in the broccoli, carrot and tomato, mix well and serve.

CHIVA-SOM'S BEAN SALAD

Another excellent change from what is expected of green salads. If you are eating Western style, you might consider this as a first course. But if you are serving good wine, I would leave out the shallots and go easier on the chillies.

SERVES 4–6

400 g (14 oz) green beans, topped and tailed and cut in 5 cm (2 inch) lengths
1 tablespoon nam pla *(fish sauce)*
8 tablespoons lemon or lime juice
2 tablespoons chopped Thai shallots
1 teaspoon palm sugar
5 small hot fresh chillies, chopped

1–2 garlic cloves, chopped
3 medium tomatoes, peeled, seeded and chopped
1 tablespoon fresh basil leaves, sliced
2 teaspoons mixed nuts, roasted

TO SERVE
lettuce and fresh coriander leaves

Mix together the beans (either raw or very lightly blanched for a few seconds in slightly salted boiling water), *nam pla*, lemon or lime juice, shallots, sugar, chillies and garlic. Fold in the tomatoes, basil and nuts.

Serve in individual lettuce leaf cups, garnished with coriander leaves.

GREEN MANGO SALAD
Yum Mamuang

One of the simplest and most popular of Thai-style salads; you can, of course, use other sour or sharp fruits – a green apple or cooking apple is the most usual substitute. Believe it or not, this makes a terrific dip or sauce for fried fish, or fish and chips. Trust me!

SERVES 4–6

3 small green mangoes, cut in fine julienne strips
1 tablespoon finely chopped garlic
1 tablespoon chopped fresh red chillies
8 tablespoons nam pla *(fish sauce)*
4 tablespoons lime juice

8 tablespoons finely chopped dry-roasted peanuts
4 tablespoons shallot strips, fried
4 tablespoons chopped garlic, fried
2 tablespoons chopped fresh coriander
3 tablespoons fresh red chillies, cut in julienne strips

Combine the prepared mango (or other fruit) with the garlic, chopped chillies, *nam pla* and lime juice. Serve it topped with the peanuts, shallot, garlic, coriander and *julienne* of chillies.

GRILLED BEEF SALAD WITH GRAPES
Pla Nuea Yaang Gub A-Ngoon

As you can see by the number of very hot chillies specified, this is planned as a very fiery salad indeed, even with the soothing effect of the grapes. In fact, everything is exaggerated, and yet it's such a delicious combination that you shouldn't allow yourself to be put off. If you don't like hot food, include fewer chillies!

Use leftover roast rib of beef or sliced grilled steak and you really have a sensational dish to serve as a summer main course, Western style. But you must take extra care to slice the lemon grass and lime leaf finely enough to be eaten with pleasure. If white Muscat grapes are in season, they work particularly well and are much better than inferior black grapes. This sophisticated dish is from Executive Chef Vitchit Mukura, of the Baan Rim Naam at The Oriental, of course.

SERVES 4–6

21 very small hot chillies
5 garlic cloves
2 teaspoons chopped coriander root, or 1 coriander plant, chopped
1 large fresh mint sprig plus 4 mint leaves
½ teaspoon salt
5 tablespoons nam pla (fish sauce)
5 tablespoons lime juice
½ teaspoon palm sugar
350 g (12 oz) cooked beef, finely sliced and cut in julienne strips

100 g (4 oz) lemon grass bulbs, very finely sliced
24 kaffir lime leaves, very finely sliced
175 g (6 oz) black grapes, halved and seeded

TO GARNISH
at least 30 small fresh mint leaves

Pound or process together the chillies, garlic, coriander, mint sprig and leaves and salt. Add the *nam pla*, lime juice and sugar; mix well.

Combine the chilli mixture with the prepared beef, lemon grass, lime leaves and grapes; toss well. Leave this to marinate for an hour or so if you like; it's much nicer served lightly chilled. Serve garnished with the mint leaves.

M.R. Thanadsri's Thai Steak Tartar
Larb Neua Thai

This is the speciality of Mom Ratchawong Thanadsri Svasti, one of Thailand's culinary icons. Although brought up in the royal palace complex, he struck out for independence early and became a famed popular singer, before channelling his interest in Thai history, culture and cuisine into a career that makes him amongst the best-known personalities on radio and television in Thailand today. This is his recipe but, in typical Thai fashion, he expects you to make your own version.

Serves 2–4

2 tablespoons rice	To Garnish
2 teaspoons chopped Thai shallots	2 teaspoons finely sliced spring onion
2 teaspoons chopped garlic	2 teaspoons finely sliced fresh chervil
1–2 fresh red chillies	
225 g (8 oz) sirloin steak, minced or	To Serve
chopped	cucumber slices
nam pla (fish sauce)	fresh mint sprigs
1–2 tablespoons lime juice or cognac	Melba toast, or rice cakes, toasted

First toast the rice grains. The simplest way is to stir-fry them over very gentle heat in a non-stick pan. When they are nicely browned, grind them finely, perhaps in a coffee grinder.

The shallots, garlic and chillies must also be roasted or, at least, browned. If you are using a pan, a very little oil might be added but a low, slow, dry heat is best, Otherwise, spread the shallots, garlic and pepper on a piece of cooking foil, fold it over to protect the ingredients and put the foil parcel under a gentle grill; they will slowly roast without burning. The chillies should be of a medium to large size, rather than the small, intense type.

Pound or process together the roasted shallots, garlic and chilli and them mix this paste evenly into the beef. Add nam pla and the lime juice or cognac (perhaps some of each if you like) and, as you mix, you will see the lime juice changing the colour of the beef. Now add up to 2 table-spoons of hot water or of hot stock to make a consistency like thick por-ridge. Work in most of the spring onions and chervil, reserving some of each as a garnish. The flavour should be sharp with lime but still showing the saltiness and flavour of the *nam pla*; add more of either to get a balance you like. Finally, bind the mixture by adding the ground, roasted rice, which gives both texture and added fragrance.

Serve garnished with the reserved spring onion and chervil and with plenty of cucumber, mint sprigs and either Melba toast or toasted rice cakes.

PORK AND HERB SALAD
Lap Moo

Simple, direct flavours here and not at all what we would think of as a salad. Essentially from the north, this is, in fact, eaten all over Thailand. This is how they teach you to prepare it at The Thai House.

SERVES 4–6

150 ml (5 fl oz) water
450 g (1 lb) lean minced pork
100 g (4 oz) pork liver, chopped
2 tablespoons lime juice
2 tablespoons ground pan-roasted rice
(page 100) or dry breadcrumbs
½ teaspoon cayenne pepper
2 teaspoons thinly sliced Thai shallots

2 spring onions, cut into 5 mm
(¼-inch) lengths
4 tablespoons chopped fresh coriander
plant, including roots
2 tablespoons nam pla (fish sauce)

TO GARNISH
30 fresh mint leaves

Heat the water and then cook the pork in it for a few minutes only until it no longer looks raw. Drain the pork, reserving the water.

In a saucepan, bring the reserved water to the boil and add the liver for a short time, just to cook it through. Drain and then combine the pork and liver with all the remaining ingredients, except the mint leaves, and mix lightly together. Serve garnished with the mint leaves.

MIXED SEAFOOD SALAD
Yam Thale

For many, this could be a gratifying and unusual main course: it's certainly an option when you want to put together something quickly on a hot summer's day. Don't forget to go easy on the shallots, or even to leave them out, if you are serving a half-decent wine.

SERVES 4–6

FOR THE DRESSING	FOR THE SALAD
2 fresh red chillies, well pounded	100 g (4 oz) cooked squid hoods
1 tablespoon chopped garlic,	(bodies), cut in 5 cm (2 inch) pieces
well pounded	225 g (8 oz) shelled, cooked prawns
1 teaspoon white or palm sugar	100 g (4 oz) cooked, shelled mussels
4 tablespoons lime juice	100 g (4 oz) cooked fish, cubed
4 tablespoons nam pla (fish sauce)	2 Chinese celery stalks or celery
	leaves and thin stalks, thickly sliced
	1 tablespoon thinly sliced Thai shallots
	1 lettuce

To make the dressing, mix together the chillies, garlic, sugar, lime juice and *nam pla*; adjust to your palate.

Cross-hatch the squid hoods, using a very sharp knife to score parallel lines into the surface and then doing the same at right angles, making a pattern of squares.

Combine all the seafood, the celery and shallots with the prepared dressing; toss gently to coat.

Tear the lettuce leaves into serving-sized cups and then arrange these on a platter. Spoon the salad into the lettuce and serve at once.

BIG SALAD WITH MEAT AND VEGETABLES
Yam Yai

Although it's usually served as a salad course with other standard dishes of a Thai meal, clearly this could become a main course.

You will find a huge variety of mixtures called *yum yai*; sometimes it will be just a mixture of vegetables or of vegetables and fruit. If you think of it as a chef's salad, that is a bit of everything you have in the refrigerator, arranged beautifully, you will have understood the principle perfectly. If we had been filming in the Thai winter, this rather superior version of *yum yai* would have been included in the Royal Banquet; but, of course, what the Thais think of as winter weather is not a lot different from the British high summer. Serve it just when you like.

SERVES 4–6

225 g (8 oz) thin rice noodles

FOR THE DRESSING
2 tablespoons chopped garlic
2 tablespoons chopped fresh red chillies
2 tablespoons chopped coriander root or plant
2 tablespoons julienne of fresh galangal
6 tablespoons nam pla (fish sauce)
4 tablespoons lime juice or cider vinegar
4 tablespoons white or palm sugar

FOR THE SALAD
225 g (8 oz) pork, boiled or roasted and thinly sliced

225 g (8 oz) chicken, boiled or roasted and thinly sliced
225 g (8 oz) shelled, cooked prawns
4 hard-boiled eggs, sliced
1 Chinese cabbage, stem removed, sliced
225 g (8 oz) peeled cucumber, thinly sliced
225 g (8 oz) tomatoes, cut in segments or thin slices
up to 50 g (2 oz) dried wood-ear fungus, soaked, drained and chopped

TO GARNISH
24 small fresh coriander sprigs
2 tablespoons fresh red chillies, cut in julienne strips
60 fresh mint leaves

Prepare the noodles. Once they're drained, cut them in 5 cm (2 inch) lengths.

Pound or process together the garlic, chillies, coriander and galangal. Stir together with the *nam pla*, lime juice or vinegar and sugar. Toss the meats, prawns and noodles in just enough of the dressing to coat them. These ingredients can be mixed together or kept separate.

On a large serving platter, make lines, curls, waves or other patterns with the noodles, meats, prawns and other ingredients, starting with a base of the cabbage. Garnish with the coriander, chillies and mint leaves, and serve the remaining dressing separately. If there were superior mangoes, papaya or pineapples in season and you were not serving them elsewhere I would not resist the temptation of including some, as is the case with almost anything else delicious and seasonal, fruit or vegetable.

ROAST AUBERGINE SALAD
Yam Ma-Kheua Yau

Don't worry too much about how much or what sort of aubergines you use, as long as they are not the purple Mediterranean type. I have used both big and small egg-shaped ones and the result was consistently delicious. The ideal weight of aubergines is about 450 g (1 lb) but allow a 25 per cent leeway without worry. To save time, slice and microwave the aubergine, and then slowly grill or barbecue it. This is much faster and just as tasty.

SERVES 4–6

2 long Thai aubergines
2 teaspoons sliced hot fresh chillies
3 tablespoons sliced Thai shallots
2–3 tablespoons nam pla (fish sauce)
4 tablespoons lime juice

1 tablespoon white or palm sugar
50 g (2 oz) minced pork, quickly fried
50 g (2 oz) cooked, shelled prawns, roughly chopped
2 tablespoons fresh mint leaves

Roast the aubergines in their skins under a slow grill, turning them regularly until they're soft throughout. Alternatively, roast them at 180°C/350°F/Gas 4 for about 45 minutes or until they're soft and the skin is beginning to brown.

Meanwhile, mix together the chillies, shallot, nam pla, lime juice and sugar.

Let the aubergines cool and then peel them and cut them in thick slices. Stir into the prepared dressing mixture, add the pork and prawns and serve garnished with the mint leaves.

Duck Salad
Larb Pied

Something for a very special meal: the very best flavour will come from buying a Barbary duck breast or *magret*. One of those will weigh more than the amount specified in the recipe, so perhaps make more and make it a main course or a spectacular first course for a large table of guests. How far it actually stretches depends on how profligate you are with the accompanying vegetables. With good wine, I recommend long and slow cooking for the shallots, so they are sweet, rather than using them raw.

The ground toasted rice adds a nuttiness to this but it can be replaced with very fine toasted breadcrumbs, if you must.

Serve this with a variety of fresh green vegetables: lightly steamed or stir-fried beans, cabbage, cucumber, asparagus, beanshoots and so on.

Serves 4–6

225 g (8 oz)boneless, skinless duck, minced

4 tablespoons lime juice

2 tablespoons thinly sliced Thai shallots

2 tablespoons coarsely chopped celery leaves

15–20 fresh mint leaves

2–3 tablespoons toasted rice grains, ground

1–2 tablespoons cayenne pepper

3 tablespoons nam pla (fish sauce)

To Serve
lettuce leaves

Cook the duck with 2 tablespoons of the lime juice in a dry wok or pan, just until it no longer looks raw.

Off the heat, mix the duck with the remaining lime juice and all the other ingredients, except the lettuce. Toss gently until well mixed. The flavour should be equally sour and salty, so adjust it to taste with *nam pla* and lime juice.

Spoon this mixture on to a serving plate lined with the lettuce leaves.

Larb Kai

This is essentially the same dish made with chicken. The major difference is that the chicken breast is minced together with its skin.

DESSERTS

A really big Thai dinner serves two styles of dessert: 'something liquid and something dry' is how it is usually described. That is likely to mean something rubbery and something in coconut milk and, frankly, few of them are to European taste, being based on mung beans or rice or water chestnuts, for instance. The easy way out of this is to offer you dozens of ways to serve bananas, with or without coconut, but that would be boring. So what I really recommend is that you do what most Thais do and serve whatever delicious and exotic fruit is in season. But here are just four truly luscious dessert ideas for the times you want to make a special effort.

STEWED BANANA IN COCONUT
Kluay Baud Tee

It is worth making the effort and paying the higher price to find the small, squarish bananas that Thais prefer for such desserts, and they must be really ripe and sweet. Failing that, three or four of the more common type will do, but they also must be properly ripe, with spotty skins and a big fragrance.

SERVES 4–6

6 sugar bananas	1 teaspoon lime juice
175 g (6 oz) palm sugar	300 ml (10 fl oz) coconut milk
½ teaspoon salt	150 ml (5 fl oz) coconut cream

Peel the bananas and cut them in quarters, lengthways. Combine the sugar, salt (which is essential), lime juice, coconut milk and cream in a pan. Stir over a gentle heat until the sugar is dissolved; then turn up the heat and cook until the mixture just comes to the boil.

Remove from the heat immediately and then add the bananas. Lower the heat and leave to simmer very gently until the fruit is softened but still firm on the outside; the mixture will curdle if you use prolonged or high heat. Spoon carefully into a serving bowl or individual bowls, with the coconut liquid, and leave until everything is just lukewarm or cold.

PUMPKIN-BAKED COCONUT CUSTARD
Sangkaya Phakthong

I know this sounds an unlikely combination but its huge popularity proves that it is perfectly delicious. This classic version comes from The Oriental Hotel in Bangkok, where the unceasing popularity of this dessert is also based on the opportunity for sensational presentation, particularly if you are able to carve pretty patterns through the pumpkin skin, before or after baking.

SERVES 6–8

4 large eggs, or 2 ducks' eggs plus 3 small hens' eggs
300 ml (10 fl oz) coconut cream
175 g (6 oz) palm or white sugar
1 small whole pumpkin, about 20 cm (8 inches) in diameter

TO SERVE
prepared tropical fruit, chilled, and/or tropical-fruit ice cream or sorbet, and/or crushed ice

Beat together the eggs, coconut cream and sugar until the sugar is dissolved. Unlike when making Western-style baked custards, it is acceptable for the mixture to be frothy; indeed, it is encouraged.

Cut the top from the pumpkin, just far enough down to expose the seeded centre. Trim the pumpkin's base, to ensure it will sit flat, but do not expose the centre. Spoon out the seeds and enough of the flesh to ensure the custard mixture will all be contained; you may like to test this a few times with an equivalent volume of water. Be careful you do not cut through the flesh at the base.

Pour the coconut-cream mixture into the pumpkin but do not replace the lid. Steam the pumpkin in a colander over gently boiling water for 20–30 minutes, or until the pumpkin flesh is cooked and the custard is set. A discreet skewer test will tell you this.

Allow to cool before removing from the heat. Serve cut in thick slices or wedges, ideally with tropical fruit or a tropically flavoured ice cream or sorbet. Although it is naturally sweeter when at cool room temperature, this does look particularly well when set atop a mound of crushed ice on which you have arranged sliced fruit.

VARIATION: For those who are calorie-conscious, Chiva-Som Health Resort has developed a modern version. For the same size pumpkin: mix together 7 egg whites, 200 ml (7 fl oz) of skimmed milk, about 5 table-spoons of apple concentrate or 50 g (2 oz) of palm or white sugar and 2 tablespoons of desiccated coconut. Cook and serve in the same way, but with less guilt.

COCONUT AND PALM SUGAR POTS

I suppose these are really a Thai version of crème caramel. If nothing else, they are by far the best of the rather rubbery and sticky Thai desserts you so often face. This combination is very acceptable to Westerners and makes an interesting contrast to tropical fruit; it is commonly made in rather small cups but you may find it easier to use ramekins.

SERVES 6

50 g (2 oz) plus 3 tablespoons
rice flour
2 tablespoons arrowroot or cornflour
900 ml (1½ pints) coconut cream
75 g (3 oz) palm sugar

6 tablespoons hot water
pinch of salt

TO SERVE
prepared tropical fruit, chilled

Blend together the 50 g (2 oz) of rice flour and the arrowroot or corn-flour and then slowly mix in 300 ml (10 fl oz) of the coconut cream.

Over gentle heat, melt the sugar, stirring as you do, and then bring it to the boil and allow it to deepen in colour but not to burn. Then add the water, mix well to dissolve and leave to cool. Blend the caramel into the rice flour mixture.

Divide the mixture evenly between six small (100–150 ml/3½–5 fl oz) ramekins. Steam or microwave until transparent; the sign that they are set. The time taken will vary enormously according to the texture of your mixture and the size of your ramekins. As an indication, they should be microwave-steamed in 6–8 minutes on medium in an 850-watt microwave. Ordinary steaming may take 30 minutes or more.

Mix the remaining coconut cream with the 3 tablespoons of rice flour and salt and divide the mixture between the ramekins. Steam or microwave again (about 6 minutes on Medium in an 850-watt oven) until the top mixture is lightly set – it will be pretty runny but you should no longer taste the rice flour. Serve lightly chilled, with tropical fruit.

JASMINE TAPIOCA WITH TROPICAL FRUIT

This is school dinners gone to heaven. More coconut I'm afraid, although you could use milk and be wimpishly less calorific. The jasmine essence is my idea, so don't be afraid to leave it out if this seems too exotic; it is just as nice without or flavoured with genuine vanilla essence. Actually, you could also use the smaller-grained sago, rather than tapioca, or even the instant types now available. These servings are quite small.

SERVES 4–6

175 g (6 oz) tapioca	*mali (jasmine essence), to taste*
1.5 litres (2½ pints) water	*(optional)*
350 g (12 oz) white or palm sugar	
pinch of salt	TO SERVE
600 ml (1 pint) coconut cream	*prepared tropical fruit, chilled*

Rinse and drain the tapioca and then bring it to the boil from cold in the water. Stir only once or twice. Reduce the heat to a gentle simmer and cook for 15–20 minutes until the tapioca is transparent, again stirring only once or twice.

Remove from the heat and leave to stand, covered, for a further 15–20 minutes, by which time the grains should be fully cooked, transparent and tender. There will usually be a few rogue ones with *al dente* centres, but don't risk overcooking the others for the sake of these few; ignore or discard them. If you are using sago, reduce timings by half.

Drain the tapioca in a colander and rinse it very well under warm running water. Dissolve two-thirds of the sugar and the salt in half the coconut cream. White sugar will give a nice pale look but, once you have the taste for palm sugar, you may want to use that and also enjoy the golden colour it gives. Flavour with the jasmine essence, if you like, being bolder than you first think; it will be diluted by the rest of the coconut sauce and the fruits. The exact amount will depend on the concentration of the brand you buy. Stir the tapioca into the coconut-cream mixture and chill lightly.

To serve, mix together the remaining coconut cream and sugar and then put this into a pretty serving bowl in the centre of an arrangement of tropical fruit – mangoes, lychees, fresh coconut … that sort of thing.

(OPPOSITE): *Jasmine Tapioca with Tropical Fruit* (TOP) *Stewed Banana in Coconut* (BELOW)

THE ROYAL BANQUET

I was lucky enough to share in a Royal Banquet to celebrate the golden anniversary of the accession of HM the King of Thailand, served in truly regal style at the palace of HRH Princess Sudhasiri Sobha in a small country palace built by her father. On that occasion, the central dish, *Khao Chae*, came with very traditional accompaniments. As this refreshing soup of jasmine-scented rice has, quite recently, found its way out of palaces and into restaurants, it can also be found accompanied by other delicacies. I have included a couple of possible alternatives here for that reason. The recipe for *Crisp-fried Beef*, for instance, is a possible substitute for the classic *Candied Dried Fish* and is much more accessible to Western palates; the *Stuffed Thai Shallots* might replace the *Fried Pickled Daikon*, and so on.

OUR ROYAL BANQUET MENU WAS:

Iced Jasmine-scented Rice
Stuffed Banana Peppers in Golden Egg Nets
Stuffed Thai Shallots
Fish and Kapi Balls
Stir-fried Pickled Daikon

Salted Fish in Egg Batter
Candied Dried Fish
Selection of Carved Fresh Fruit, Vegetables and Herbs
Mangoes with Sweet Sticky Rice

ICED JASMINE-SCENTED RICE
Khao Chae

Khao Chae is a perfect example of the trouble royal Thai cooks once took to tempt jaded appetites in hot weather: a soup of iced and scented rice with a selection of intricately prepared accompaniments to give maximum contrast of flavour and texture. It was apparently invented in the nineteenth century, when ice was so rare that King Chulalongkorn's household had to import it from Singapore. A simpler version of cooked rice served in cool, unscented water can often be found in market places, especially about Petburi, where this king had a summer palace; argument rages about which version came first.

Frankly, if you have used the right rice, this is just as nice without the jasmine flavouring; you can always sprinkle it with a few edible flowers of some kind. Rosewater and rose petals are a delicious alternative to jasmine and much easier, because rosewater is much more commonly available.

If you are lucky enough to grow scented jasmine that has not been sprayed, here is what you do instead of using jasmine essence. Boil the water, first also having filtered it if you use a water purifier. When it is cool, put it into a shallow container, so that it has maximum surface, and carefully float jasmine blossoms face-down on it; if they are really strongly scented, 12 blossoms should do. Cover tightly and leave at room temperature. Check the flavour and, if it is not strong enough, remove the flowers and add more; don't leave the blooms in too long or a stale flavour develops.

Treat this voluptuous rice as a soup, enjoying scented spoonfuls as a grateful contrast to the other goodies. It is served with a selection of stuffed vegetables and other fried foods, examples of which are in this chapter, as part of a summer menu; I like it with almost any meal and in any season.

Serves 4–6

225 g (8 oz) Thai fragrant (jasmine) rice
½ teaspoon mali (jasmine essence)

12 ice cubes, roughly cracked
about 450 ml (15 fl oz) cold water
flower petals, to garnish

First rinse the rice in cold running water and then leave it to soak in well salted cold water for 3 hours. Rinse in running water again.

Bring a large saucepan of water to the boil and cook the rice for about 5 minutes until it looks like fish eggs: transparent on the outside but opaque in the middle. Rinse very well in cold running water.

Wrap the rice lightly in fine cheesecloth or muslin and steam it over boiling water until it's cooked, which should only take a few minutes. It shouldn't be sticky but, to be certain, tip it out on to a large platter and separate the grains. Cool, cover and then chill. You can simply cook the rice your usual way and then rinse it continuously under cold running water until it's clear, but this isn't half as much fun.

When you are ready to serve, that is when you have also prepared the fiddly accompaniments described in this chapter, crush the ice cubes and mix them into the rice. Flavour the measured water with *mali*. Stir it into the rice and ice mixture, using just enough so the rice floats but is not drowned; it should look like a thick rice soup but, if you have prepared the rice properly, the water will remain crystal clear. Or you can serve the prepared rice, flavoured water and crushed ice separately, allowing guests to make a texture they prefer.

STUFFED BANANA PEPPERS
Prik Sod Sai Rum

Banana peppers are long, pointed sweet peppers. A terrific appetizer or first course, these stuffed and fried peppers are also one of the accompaniments to *Iced Jasmine-scented Rice* (page 112); it then becomes part of a main-course.

The quantity of batter here should be enough to coat a batch of stuffed peppers and a batch of *Stuffed Thai Shallots* (page 116). Use half if you are making just one or the other, of course.

SERVES 4–8

4–8 yellow or green sweet banana peppers, maximum 10 cm (4 inches) long
100 g (4 oz) minced pork
100 g (4 oz) raw, shelled prawns, finely chopped
salt
1 teaspoon black peppercorns, roughly crushed
1 teaspoon chopped garlic
1 dessertspoon chopped coriander plant, including root
vegetable oil, for frying
2–3 teaspoons nam pla (fish sauce)

1–2 teaspoons palm sugar
1 egg, beaten
2 tablespoons dry-roasted peanuts, finely chopped, or 1 tablespoon crunchy peanut butter

FOR THE FRYING BATTER
225 g (8 oz) self-raising flour
about 300 ml (10 fl oz) cold water
2 teaspoons palm sugar
1 teaspoon salt
2 tablespoons vegetable oil
finely chopped chillies, chilli powder or Tabasco sauce, to taste

Slice off the stalk end of the peppers at an angle and reserve them to use as lids. Wash the seeds out of the peppers. Mix together the pork and the prawns (using your hands is easiest).

Fry the salt, peppercorns, garlic and coriander in a little oil until fragrant and then stir in the pork and prawn mixture evenly. Cook through, add the *nam pla* and sugar and then remove from the heat. Mix in the egg and the peanuts or peanut butter. Stuff the peppers evenly; they do not need to be full.

To make the batter, whisk the ingredients together as quickly as you can to make a thick batter (lumps don't matter).

Dip the peppers into the batter, using some of it to reattach the lid, and then fry them in more hot oil until the filling is cooked and the batter is golden brown.

Traditionally, each would be wrapped in an egg net. I know that is asking a bit much in these busy days, but if you have the time, the recipe is as follows.

GOLDEN EGG NETS
Pae Kai

Two eggs will make four or five nets in a 20 cm (8 inch) non-stick pan, and each of these can be cut to wrap around two stuffed banana peppers. That is, two eggs can make nets for up to 10 peppers if you wrap them as a cone. You can also wrap each pepper completely as a neat parcel, using a full net per pepper.

When first making these, allow extra eggs for practice and luck. If one or some of the egg can be from a duck, the flavour and colour are enhanced.

Lightly beat the eggs together and then put them through a sieve to remove lumps. Put this mixture into a deep container into which you can put a hand. Heat the pan over medium heat. Holding the container of eggs close to the edge of the pan, dip your fingers deep into the egg mixture and then drizzle the egg from your fingertips over the pan, shaking them slightly from side to side as you do. Drizzle at different angles until you have a lacy effect all over the base of the pan. Don't turn the net over, but remove it with a large spatula and then make the next one.

For those with most time and assured skills, the ultimate version of this recipe is to make steamed peppers and to put a little oil in the bottom of the pan when making the egg nets. When each is ready and lightly crisp and golden underneath, put a steamed pepper into the centre of the net, fold the net into a neat package over it, and then turn that over and fry until crisp. Drain and cool. Do it again. You can see why these are served cool rather than hot!

VARIATION: STEAMED STUFFED BANANA PEPPERS

When serving these at the palace of HRH Princess Sudhasiri Sobha, the chef steamed the stuffed peppers before wrapping them in fried egg nets, giving a lighter texture and lower fat content. To follow this example, open the banana peppers lengthways, keeping the stem attached, and then remove the seeds and what membranes there are. Mix together the pork, prawns, coriander, garlic, white pepper and *nam pla*; go easy on the white pepper as it is more fiery than black and can easily overpower. There were neither palm sugar nor peanuts in this version but you can add them, if you like.

Stuff the peppers evenly and reshape them. Steam them on a platter over simmering water until cooked through, which will take 15–30 minutes, according to your type of steamer. In a microwave, these are best steamed gently, lightly covered. Cook the full batch on Medium in an 850-watt microwave for 10 minutes and then check and cook on in 2-minute bursts until done. Let them cool completely before wrapping them in their egg nets.

VARIATION: STUFFED THAI SHALLOTS (HOM YAD SAI)

Individual shallots or, perhaps, small onions can be stuffed with the same mixture as the Peppers. If you are already using that recipe and want a contrasting taste for your selection, add a little chopped fresh galangal and lemon grass to the stuffing and use thick coconut cream instead of ground peanuts or peanut butter.

Microwave or boil the shallots or onions until they are sweet and tender and then remove the centre, chopping that and adding it to the stuffing. Stuff them and then dip them into the frying batter and fry them as for the peppers.

CRISP-FRIED BEEF
Neua Khem Phad

A real East-meets-West dish, shredded corned (salt) beef, deep-fried, flavoured with sugar and salt and served with fried garlic and shallots – a local version of the USA's *Red Flannel Hash*. Amazing really, and amazingly popular with those who have discovered or rediscovered it.

The corned beef must be tender enough to be shredded when pulled with two forks, thus canned – as in the original recipe – is best.

SERVES 4–6

vegetable oil, for frying
450 g (1 lb) canned corned beef, shredded
2 or more tablespoons caster sugar

6 garlic cloves, sliced and fried
3 Thai shallots, sliced and fried
salt

Heat about 2 cm (¾ inch) of vegetable oil in a frying-pan in which the shredded beef will make a layer of about the same depth. Don't be manic about this but, to get the right effect, there has to be enough oil and enough space for the beef to get at it. A small, thick layer simply won't crispen.

Fry the beef, turning it from time to time, until it has absorbed most of the oil; then add the sugar and salt to taste and lower the heat. Continue frying, without stirring too often, until each shred is crisp.

Remove the beef from the heat, take out a spoonful and let it cool before tasting to ensure it is, indeed, crisp. If not, continue cooking the panful. Finally, drain well and serve topped with the garlic and shallots.

(OVERLEAF, FROM LEFT): *Stuffed Banana Peppers in Golden Egg Nets, Khao Chae, Mangoes with Sweet Sticky Rice and Fish and Kapi Balls*

FISH AND KAPI BALLS
Kapi Chuep Kai Tod

The unusual flavours of *krachai* (wild or white ginger) and of *kapi* (shrimp paste) combine with fish, coconut and lemon grass to make tiny explosions of fascinating effect. Exactly the right thing to get your appetite going. If *kra-chai* is not available, fresh galangal with a little fresh ginger might do. The correct fish is catfish, but any solid fish, devoid of bones, is fine. Time is probably the hardest ingredient to find in this recipe, as the balls should ideally be half the size of marbles.

SERVES 6–8

225 g (8 oz) krachai *(wild or white ginger)*, *peeled*
100 g *(4 oz) lemon grass bulbs*
100 g *(4 oz) highest-quality* kapi *(shrimp paste)*
50 g *(2 oz) Thai shallots*

225 g *(8 oz) boneless, skinless fish, grilled*
100 g *(4 oz) palm sugar*
200 ml *(8 fl oz) coconut cream*
2 eggs
vegetable oil, for deep-frying

Pound or process together the *krachai*, lemon grass, *kapi*, shallots, fish and sugar, until you have a really smooth paste.

Heat the coconut cream over medium heat until the fat starts to separate. Add the prepared mixture, reduce the heat to low and cook, stirring constantly, until the mixture comes away from the side of a pan, as though you were making choux pastry; the coconut oil should be separating again, too. Leave to cool.

Once cold, form into balls half the size of marbles and arrange on a flat surface. Once the balls have dried a little, which prevents them from sticking together, proceed with the next stage or freeze or refrigerate them.

Beat the eggs very lightly, so they do not froth. Dip the balls into this and deep-fry them until they're golden brown. Drain them on kitchen paper and arrange them beautifully. They are eaten cold or warm, according to your organizational ability or number of kitchen staff.

STIR-FRIED PICKLED DAIKON
Hua Chai Po Pad Kai

The flavour target here is a light salt-sweetness, obtained by buying only the highest-quality salted *daikon* (Chinese radish); if in doubt, soak it in a few changes of water.

SERVES 4–6

350 g (12 oz) pickled daikon	*1 ducks' egg and 1 hens' egg,*
6–8 tablespoons vegetable oil	*or 2 hens' eggs*
2 teaspoons palm sugar	*salt*

Carefully slice the pickled *daikon* and then cut it in fine *julienne* strips. Heat the oil and then stir-fry the *daikon* until it's heated through. Add the sugar and continue stir-frying until this is absorbed. There should be a slight excess of oil remaining; if not add a tablespoon or more or the eggs will not cook. Lightly mix together the eggs and pour over the *daikon*. Let the egg begin to set for a few seconds and then mix and stir all together. Correct the seasoning with more sugar or salt and then heap on to a platter. It is good to serve this hot during the meal, if you can.

VARIATION: A more robust version is made by grating the pickled *daikon*. Then fry about 175 g (6 oz) of small pork fat cubes, until they are crisp and have rendered most of their fat. Pour away most of the fat to use for another purpose; drain and reserve the crisp fat cubes. In the remaining rendered pork fat, fry a tablespoon of chopped garlic until it is golden brown and then add the *daikon*, reserved crisp pork fat and palm sugar. When heated through, continue by adding the eggs as above; correct the seasoning and then serve.

SALTED FISH IN EGG BATTER
Pla Kem Chup Pang Tod

An acquired taste, but many aspire to and achieve a great love of such things. If you are one of them, simply cut Thai salted fish – ideally, salted king fish – into bite-sized pieces, dip them into lightly beaten egg, deep-fry and then enjoy.

CANDIED DRIED FISH
Pla Wan

And yet another challenge to Western palates: not the crispness or the sweetness or the saltiness, but the rather special flavour that Thai salted fish develops. Here, salted and dried grouper is finely sliced, deep-fried and then served in a caramelized sauce of *nam pla* (fish sauce), palm sugar and water. For two generous handfuls of the prepared dried fish, 225 g (8 oz) of palm sugar to about 3 tablespoons each of *nam pla* and of water is about right. This really is an acquired taste.

SELECTION OF CARVED FRESH FRUIT, VEGETABLES AND HERBS
Pak Tang Tang

As well as the cooked accompaniments to the scented rice, this banquet meal also includes a selection of raw vegetables and herbs, as you might expect. Wild ginger, *krachai*, is considered important but the world does not end if you do not serve it; it should be peeled and sliced or carved into such shapes as trees. Carved cucumbers, spring onions with fringes curled in iced water and green mangoes carved into leaf shapes would be expected to make an appearance, too. Provided only that you create a continuous contrast of texture and flavour, and that you can make your accompaniments a treat for the eye as well as for the palate, the real choice is up to you.

MANGOES WITH SWEET STICKY RICE
Khao Neow Ma-Muang

The people of northern Thailand have a passion for eating sticky rice with a special type of mango that can be enjoyed whilst still green and crisp. But ripe mango served with coconut-flavoured sticky rice is much more sophisticated and more easily copied.

The preferred variety of mango is the *ok-rong*, which is particularly sweet, fragrant and nicely teardrop-shaped. They are peeled and carved, fluted or sliced; two halves make a nice portion for one. The bigger mangoes more commonly available elsewhere will probably serve two people each. The amount of rice I suggest is rather less than that probably enjoyed by Thais; if you are serving this combination after a meal in which rice is less featured than in this banquet, you can increase it. Everything should be at room temperature, or only very lightly chilled, to get maximum flavour.

SERVES 6

225 g (8 oz) uncooked sticky rice
300 ml (10 fl óz) coconut cream
100 g (4 oz) sugar or palm sugar

1–2 teaspoons salt
6 small or 3 large mangoes

Cook the rice as described on page 22. Meanwhile, take half the coconut cream and flavour it with half or more of the sugar and salt. It should be quite highly flavoured, as the rice will not be seasoned. Pour this on to the cooked rice whilst it is still warm and let the rice absorb the flavour, without stirring or mixing too much. Let it cool and then add more sugar or salt, according to taste.

Peel the mangoes and carve or slice them. An easier route is merely to cut off each side or cheek as close as possible to the flat stone and then to cut a criss-cross into the flesh, almost down to the skin. Then gently turn each mango half inside-out and the cubes of flesh will stand out on the inverted skin. Arrange the prepared rice and mangoes on a platter or individual serving plates. Combine the remaining coconut cream and sugar and serve this as a pouring sauce.

WHERE TO LEARN TO COOK THAI IN THAILAND

When researching this book, I looked to Thailand's established hotels and cookery schools to tell me much of what I wanted to know. It might seem from first impressions that because many of these establishments are run by managers and chefs from Europe they are out of touch with Thailand's heritage. The reality is that the Europeans work closely with Thai colleagues who have great culinary knowledge and experience, and the combination of the Europeans' fascination for Thai food and their Thai colleagues' professional expertise means that you will often get more original and interesting food in a large hotel than in small restuarants, which are apt to bend to customer whims.

This is by no means true everywhere and judgements are too often clouded by not appreciating the national pleasure in novelty – a variation or new-seeming dish will be applauded by Thais but debunked by Europeans who incorrectly expect Thailand to be some sort of static culinary museum for their personal exploration.

In general, provided you give plenty of notice and are prepared to pay for ingredients (at the very least) it is always worth phoning in advance to any hotel where you are staying to ask if lessons might be organized, or if you might visit the kitchens. There are opportunites everywhere – they even say there's a backpackers' cookery school on Ko Samui ...

The hotels and cookery schools featured are as follows.

The Oriental, Bangkok

The Oriental celebrates its 120th anniversary in 1996 and, once managed by the son of the celebrated Anna Leonowens of *The King and I* fame, it is one of the most famous and honoured hotels in the world. Executive Chef Norbert Kostner is a major consultant to HM the King and Vitchit Mukura, Executive Chef of the hotel's Baan Rim Naam restaurant, demonstrates the Oriental's style of Thai cookery all around the world.

The Oriental's cookery school, across the river from the hotel, operates daily and weekly courses which combine instruction with hands-on experience.

Tel: (66 2) 437 6211
Fax: (66 2) 439 7587

The Beaufort Sukhothai, Bangkok

Although surrounded by high-rise office buildings the floating pavilion of the Sukhothai's Thai restaurant seems serenely of another world. Sven Krauss is Executive Chef here and Sous Chef Vira Sanguanwong has been cooking professionally for over 25 years and yet they regularly put recipes offered by the families of their kitchen staff on the menu.

Their excellent book *The Food of Thailand* is published by Periplus editions.

The Chiva-Som International Health Resort, Hua Hin

This is Thailand's first health resort and one of the few in Asia. As well as having his own organic garden growing Thai and European ingredients, the hotel's Australian Executive Chef Andrew Jacka works hard with Executive Sous Chef Suphan Hemchayarti to develop delicious lower-fat versions of traditional dishes. You'll hear much more about this fascinating place.

Andrew Jacka gives free classes in lower-fat Thai cookery most Saturdays, but can be persuaded to do something special if you are there at other times, particularly for groups.

Tel: (66 32) 536 536
Fax: (66 32) 511 615

Tongsai Bay Cottages and Hotel, Ko Samui

Piengchom Darbanand began her culinary career cooking privately for senior members of the Thai Royal Family. Now she divides her time between the restaurants she oversees in Bangkok and this idyllic resort on the island of Ko Samui.

Much of the accommodation has proper baths outide on the terraces – quite the most delicious way of eating crabs and mangoes while watching the sun go down.

Amari Rincome, Chiang Mai

The north is where the kingdom of Thailand has its real roots in everything from traditional crafts and entertainments to culinary genius. The Amari is close to the old walls of Chiang Mai, perfectly set for exploring the fascinating food markets which reveal how different ingredients are up here from those of Bangkok.

The Wandee Culinary School

Run by Professor Wandee (her name means 'good day'), this place also specializes in related arts: fruit and vegetable carving, flower arranging and making floral decorations. The Professor and many of her instructors also teach at the pestigious culinary school operated by and for the Royal Palace.

Fax: (66 2) 580 9522

The Thai House

The Thai House is situated on a *klong* in the country, about 45 minutes by boat from The Oriental. Although you can visit for the day, there is also accommodation for a small numbre which allows you to go to local markets and experience near-rural life whilst learning about and then eating Thai home cooking from an excellent teacher.

Tel: (66 2) 280 0740
Fax: (66 2) 280 0741

Acknowledgements

This book and the accompanying tv series would not have been possible without the sensational help of Mom Ratchawong Thanadsri Svasti and his son Mom Luang Sirichalerm Svasti. M.R. Thanadsri was brought up in one of the royal palaces and then rather unexpectedly became Thailand's best-known musical and culinary celebrity. He has a daily radio programme with an estimated 8 million listeners, regular cookery slots on television and edits or writes widely on related topics. M.L. Siri Chalerm is a charming restaurateur and businessman of note. Between them they opened doors into beach huts and palaces throughout Thailand.

We had exceptional help from The Oriental, especially from Jonas Schuermann and Andrew Jordan and thank the hotel's legendary General Manager Kurt Wachtveitl for his support and hospitality.

Needless to say, we are also grateful for the help and advice of the Tourist Authority of Thailand and Thai Airways, particularly their offices in Sydney, Australia. And, as ever, you can do little in Thailand without the help and enthusiasm of Bacall, Harris Associates in London.

126

INDEX